LOVE TO KNIT SOCKS

TABLE OF CONTENTS

Introduction

In this book we have curated several unique sock patterns featuring a wide range of knitting styles and techniques. With each design, you will find an overview of the techniques and styles used in the sock. This allows you to decide which sock you want to tackle at a glance. We have also scattered some tips throughout the book to improve or help with your sock knitting adventure. Below is some information to get you started.

GAUGE

While gauge is an important component in making sure socks fit, most sock knitters do not make large gauge swatches. However, once you have completed a few inches of knitting, it is good practice to count the number of stitches and rounds you have near the center of your work, and compare that to the stated gauge on your pattern.

If there are fewer stitches and/or rounds than indicated in the Gauge section in the pattern, your needles are too large—you should start over with smaller needles. If there are more stitches and/or rounds than indicated in the Gauge section in the pattern, your tension is too tight, and you may want to try again with larger needles.

Because socks are not fitted, a small variation should not prevent you from wearing your socks. If there's a large difference, you can adjust your needles until the correct gauge is achieved.

READING PATTERN INSTRUCTIONS

Before beginning a pattern, look through it to make sure you are familiar with the abbreviations and techniques that are used.

Some patterns may be written for more than one size. In this case, the smallest size is given first and others are placed in parentheses. When only one number is given, it applies to all sizes.

You may wish to highlight the numbers for the size you are making before beginning. It is also helpful to place a self-sticking note on the pattern to mark any changes made while working the pattern.

MEASURING

To measure a piece, lay it flat on a smooth surface. Take the measurement in the middle of the piece. For example, measure the length of a foot or leg two inches or so away from the fold, not near the edges which can curve or draw in.

T0321281

WORKING FROM CHARTS

A chart will often be provided as a visual representation of a color or stitch pattern. Each cell of the chart represents one stitch. A key is given indicating the yarn color or stitch represented by each color or symbol in the cell.

The row number is at the edge of the chart where that row begins. If the number is at the right, the row is a right-side row and the chart row is read from right to left; if the number is at the left, the row is a wrong-side row and the chart row is read from left to right.

When working in rounds, every row on the chart is a right-side row and is read from right to left.

USE OF ZERO

In patterns that include various sizes, zeros are sometimes necessary. For example, k0 (0, 1) means if you are making the smallest or middle size, you would do nothing, and if you are making the largest size, you would k1.

METRIC CONVERSION CHART

INCHES INTO MILLIMETERS & CENTIMETERS (Rounded off slightly)

inches	mm	cm	inches	cm	inches	cm	inches	cm
1/8	3	0.3	5	12.5	21	53.5	38	96.5
1/4	6	0.6	5 1/2	14	22	56	39	99
3/8	10	1	6	15	23	58.5	40	101.5
1/2	13	1.3	7	18	24	61	41	104
5/8	15	1.5	8	20.5	25	63.5	42	106.5
3/4	20	2	9	23	26	66	43	109
7/8	22	2.2	10	25.5	27	68.5	44	112
1	25	2.5	11	28	28	71	45	114.5
1 1/4	32	3.2	12	30.5	29	73.5	46	117
1 1/2	38	3.8	13	33	30	76	47	119.5
1 3/4	45	4.5	14	35.5	31	79	48	122
2	50	5	15	38	32	81.5	49	124.5
2 1/2	65	6.5	16	40.5	33	84	50	127
3	75	7.5	17	43	34	86.5		
3 1/2	90	9	18	46	35	89		
4	100	10	19	48.5	36	91.5		
4 1/2	115	11.5	20	51	37	94		

KNITTING NEEDLES CONVERSION CHART

Canada/U.S.	0	1	2	3	4	5	6	7	8	9	10	10½	11	13	15
Metric (mm)	2	2¼	2¾	3¼	3½	3¾	4	4½	5	5½	6	6½	8	9	10

KNIT STANDARD ABBREVIATIONS

approx . . . . approximately
beg . . . . begin/begins/beginning
CC . . . . contrasting color
ch . . . . chain stitch
cm . . . . centimeter(s)
cn . . . . cable needle
dec(s) . . . . decrease/decreases/decreasing
dpn(s) . . . . double-point needle(s)
g . . . . gram(s)
inc(s) . . . . . . increase/increases/increasing
k . . . . knit
k2tog . . . . knit 2 stitches together
kfb . . . . knit in front and back
kwise . . . . knitwise
LH . . . . left hand
m . . . . meter(s)
MC . . . . main color
mm . . . . millimeter(s)
oz . . . . ounce(s)

p . . . . purl
p2tog . . . . purl 2 stitches together
pat(s) . . . . pattern(s)
pm . . . . place marker
psso . . . . pass slipped stitch over
pwise . . . . purlwise
rem . . . . remain/remains/remaining
rep(s) . . . . repeat(s)
rev St st . . . . reverse stockinette stitch
RH . . . . right hand
rnd(s) . . . . round(s)
RS . . . . right side(s)
skp . . . . . slip 1 knitwise, knit 1, pass slipped stitch over—a left-leaning decrease
sk2p . . . . . . slip 1 knitwise, knit 2 together, pass slipped stitch over the stitch from the knit-2-together decrease— a left-leaning double decrease
sl . . . . slip

sl 1 kwise . . . . slip 1 knitwise
sl 1 pwise . . . . slip 1 purlwise
sl st(s) . . . . slip stitch(es)
sm . . . . . . slip marker from LH to RH needle
ssk . . . . slip 2 stitches, 1 at a time, knitwise; knit these stitches together through the back loops—a left-leaning decrease
st(s) . . . . stitch(es)
St st . . . . stockinette stitch
tbl . . . . through the back loop
tog . . . . together
WS . . . . wrong side(s)
wyib . . . . with yarn in back
wyif . . . . with yarn in front
yd(s) . . . . yard(s)
yfwd . . . . yarn forward
yo (yo's) . . . . yarn over(s)

TURKISH CAST-ON

Step 1: Hold both needles parallel and put a slip knot onto a dpn.

Hold 2 dpns together, with the slip knit on the bottom needle. From behind the needles, wrap yarn loosely around both needles for half the total number of stitches required, ending with yarn behind both needles.

A

Step 2: Using a third dpn, knit into loops on needle on top across.

B

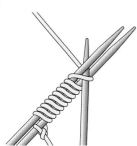

Step 3: Turn so bottom needle is on top. Undo slip knot, knit into loops across to complete Round 1.

D

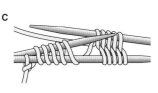

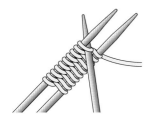

Step 4: Round 2: Divide stitches over 3 or 4 dpns and continue following pattern.

E

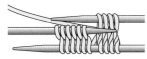

MAGIC LOOP METHOD

Use a circular needle at least 30 inches in length. Stitches are knit from one end of the needle to the other end while maintaining a loop of cable between one half of the stitches and the other half. When half of the stitches have been knit, turn work and complete the round on the other half.

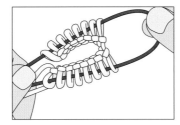

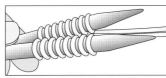

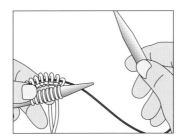

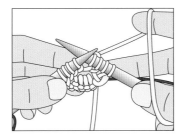

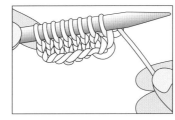

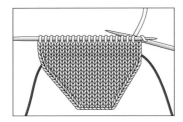

KITCHENER STITCH

This method of weaving with a tapestry needle is used for the toes of socks and flat seams. To weave the edges together and form an unbroken line of stockinette stitch, divide all stitches evenly onto two knitting needles—one behind the other. Thread yarn into tapestry needle. Hold needles with wrong sides together and work from right to left as follows:

Step 1: Insert tapestry needle into first stitch on front needle as to purl. Draw yarn through stitch, leaving stitch on knitting needle.

Step 2: Insert tapestry needle into the first stitch on the back needle as to knit. Draw yarn through stitch, leaving stitch on knitting needle.

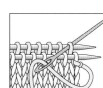

Step 3: Insert tapestry needle into the first stitch on the front needle as to knit. Draw yarn through stitch and slip stitch off knitting needle.

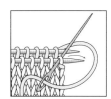

Step 4: Insert tapestry needle into the next stitch on same (front) needle as to purl. Draw yarn through stitch, leaving stitch on knitting needle.

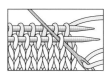

Step 5: Insert tapestry needle into the first stitch on the back needle as to purl. Draw yarn through stitch and slip stitch off knitting needle.

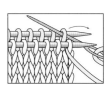

Step 6: Insert tapestry needle into the next stitch on same (back) needle as to knit. Draw yarn through stitch, leaving stitch on knitting needle.

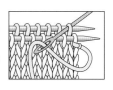

Repeat Steps 3–6 until one stitch is left on each needle. To finish, insert tapestry needle in front stitch as to knit, draw yarn through stitch and slip stitch off knitting needle; insert tapestry needle in back stitch as to purl, draw yarn through stitch and slip stitch off knitting needle. Fasten off. Woven stitches should be the same size as adjacent knitted stitches.

Blue Spiral Rib

Design by Lena Skvagerson

OVERVIEW:

♡ Top-down construction

♡ Lateral braid

♡ Heelless

♡ Spiral rib tube sock

♡ Rounded/spiral toe

♡ Cinched toe closure

If you are new to sock knitting, perhaps you want to start your adventure with these socks that don't require a tricky heel to fit your feet.

SKILL LEVEL
Easy

SIZE
Woman's small (medium, large); to fit shoe size 5 to 6 (7 to 8, 9 to 10)

Instructions are given for the smallest size, with larger sizes in parentheses. When only one number is given, it applies to all sizes.

FINISHED MEASUREMENTS
Foot Circumference: 7 (8, 9) inches

Sock Length: Approx 18 (19, 20) inches

MATERIALS
- Expression Fiber Arts Resilient Sock (fingering weight; 100% superwash merino; 400 yds/115g per skein): 1 skein seabreeze
- Size 1½ (2.5mm) double-point needles or size needed to obtain gauge
- Removable stitch marker

1 SUPER FINE

GAUGE
32 sts and 36 rows = 4 inches/10cm in St st.

To save time, take time to check gauge.

PATTERN NOTES
The yarn overs and decreases worked every round cause the fabric to bias to the right as you work.

Spiral Pattern is a multiple of 8 stitches.

The unique nature and rib pattern of this sock mean you do not need to work any sort of heel. It's not a mistake that the heel was left out.

SOCK
Make 2.

CUFF
Loosely cast on 56 (64, 72) sts. Divide sts among 3 dpns. Pm on first st of rnd and join to work in the rnd.

Rnds 1 and 2: Knit.

Rnd 3: *K2, p2; rep from * around.

Rep Rnd 3 until piece measures 1½ inches.

Braid rnd: *Reach behind first st and knit into back of 2nd st, then knit into front of first st, dropping both sts from LH needle, slip last st from RH needle back to LH needle; rep from * to end, leaving last st on RH (do not slip it back to LH needle). Join end of braid to beg as follows: Insert RH needle underneath both legs of first braid st below LH needle and lift them onto LH needle, then knit them tog tbl; pass the 2nd st on the RH needle over the first st.

Next rnd: Knit.

LEG
Spiral Pattern
Set-up rnd: *K3, yo, k3, k2tog; rep from * around.

Rnd 1: *K3, yo, k1-tbl (yo from previous rnd), k2, k2tog; rep from * around.

Rep Rnd 1 until piece measures approx 16½ (17½, 18½) inches, or to 1½ inches less than desired length.

TOE
Rnd 1: *K3, k1-tbl (yo from previous rnd), k2, k2tog; rep from * around—49 (56, 63) sts.

Rnd 2: *K3, yo, k2, k2tog; rep from * around.

Rnd 3: *K3, k1-tbl (yo from previous rnd), k1, k2tog; rep from * around—42 (48, 54) sts.

Rnd 4: *K3, yo, k1, k2tog; rep from * around.

Rnd 5: *K3, k1-tbl (yo from previous rnd), k2tog; rep from * around—35 (40, 45) sts.

Rnd 6: *K3, yo, k2tog; rep from * around.

Rnd 7: *K1, ssk, k1-tbl (yo from previous rnd), k1; rep from * around—28 (32, 36) sts.

Rnd 8: Knit.

Rnd 9: *K2, k2tog; rep from * around—21 (24, 27) sts.

Rnd 10: Knit.

Rnd 11: *K1, k2tog; rep from * around—14 (16, 18) sts.

Rnd 12: Knit.

Rnd 13: *K2tog; rep from * around—7 (8, 9) sts.

Cut yarn leaving an 8-inch tail. Thread tail through rem sts and pull tight to close.

FINISHING
Weave in all ends. ●

TIP:
When beginning the cuff, cast on using a needle 2 to 3 sizes larger, then slip your stitches onto the correct size of double-point needles when setting up to knit your first round.

Ribbed Anklets

Design by E.J. Slayton

The standard setup of these socks will have
them flying off your needles.

OVERVIEW:

♡ Top-down construction

♡ 2x2 rib leg and instep

♡ Slip stitch heel flap

♡ Standard gusset

♡ Wedge toe

♡ Kitchener stitch

SKILL LEVEL

Intermediate

SIZE

Woman's small (medium, large)

Instructions are given for smallest size, with larger sizes in parentheses. When only 1 number is given, it applies to all sizes.

FINISHED MEASUREMENTS

Foot circumference: Approx 8½ (9, 9½) inches

Cuff: Approx 2½ inches high

MATERIALS

- Lana Grossa Meilenweit Merino Hand-Dyed sock yarn (fingering weight; 80% merino/20% nylon; 357 yds/95g per skein): 1 skein Tapi #408

1 SUPER FINE

- Size 1 (2.25mm) double-point needles (set of 4) or size needed to obtain gauge
- Stitch marker

GAUGE

15 sts and 19 rnds = 2 inches/5cm in St st.

To save time, take time to check gauge.

SPECIAL ABBREVIATIONS

Purl front and back (pfb): Purl the next stitch but do not remove the stitch from the left knitting needle. Insert the right knitting needle behind the left knitting needle and purl again into the back of the same stitch. Slip the original stitch off the left knitting needle—1 st inc.

PATTERN NOTES

Slip all stitches purlwise with yarn on wrong side of fabric.

You can work the leg to a longer length, keeping in mind it means you may need more yarn than stated in Materials list.

SOCK

Make 2.

LEG

Cast on 64 (68, 72) sts. Join without twisting, dividing sts on 3 needles. Mark beg of rnd.

Rnd 1: P1, *k2, p2; rep from * to last 3 sts, k2, p1.

Rep Rnd 1 until top measures approx 2½ inches, ending with k2, p2.

Arrange sts with last 32 (34, 36) sts on 1 needle for heel; divide rem sts between 2 needles for instep.

HEEL FLAP

Turn and purl across heel sts, inc 1 st at center back with a pfb—33 (35, 37) sts.

Row 1 (RS): Sl 1, *k1, sl 1; rep from * across.

Row 2: Purl.

Rep Rows 1 and 2 until there are 16 (17, 18) loops on each edge of heel flap, ending with Row 1.

Turn Heel

Row 1 (WS): P19 (20, 21), p2tog, p1, turn.

Row 2: Sl 1, k6, k2tog, k1, turn.

Note: There is now a gap between sts at each turning point.

Row 3: Sl 1, purl to 1 st before gap, p2tog, p1, turn.

Row 4: Sl 1, knit to 1 st before gap, k2tog, k1, turn.

SOCK KNITTING METHODS:

There are several sock knitting methods. Among them are knitting with double pointed needles (dpns), short circular sock needles, magic loop, two at a time and even knitting one sock inside another. The patterns written in this book are written for those preferring to use double-pointed needles. However, if you are familiar with other knitting methods, you can use them instead.

For example, if your preference is magic loop, you will arrange your stitches so that your instep stitches (front) are on one side of your cable and the heel/sole stitches (back) are on the opposite.

As your skills develop it may be fun to experiment with other methods to see which one you like the best. Choose a pattern with basic elements and an easy stitch pattern, like this one. That will allow you to focus on the method rather than the intricacies of a complicated pattern.

Rep Rows 3 and 4 until all sts have been worked, ending with Row 4—19 (21, 21) sts rem.

GUSSET

With needle containing heel sts, pick up and knit 16 (17, 18) sts in loops along edge of heel flap (Needle 1); work 32 (34, 36) instep sts onto 1 needle maintaining pat (Needle 2); pick up and knit 16 (17, 18) sts along left edge of heel flap, then knit 9 (10, 10) heel sts onto same needle (Needle 3)—83 (89, 93) sts.

Note: New beg of rnd is at center of heel.

Rnd 1: Knit Needle 1; work in pat across instep sts; knit Needle 3.

Rnd 2: Knit to last 3 sts on Needle 1, k2tog, k1; work in pat across instep sts; on Needle 3, k1, ssk, knit to end.

Rnds 3–18 (20, 20): Rep Rnds 1 and 2—65 (69, 73) sts.

Next rnd: Work around in established pat, dec 1 st at beg of rnd—64 (68, 72) sts.

FOOT

Continue to work even until foot measures approx 1¾ inches less than desired length. Discontinue instep pat.

TOE

Rnd 1: Knit to last 3 sts on Needle 1, k2tog, k1; **Needle 2:** k1, ssk, knit to last 3 sts, k2tog, k1; **Needle 3:** k1, ssk, knit to end.

Rnd 2: Knit around.

Rep Rnds 1 and 2 until 32 (32, 36) sts rem, ending with Rnd 1. Work Needle 1 sts onto Needle 3. Cut yarn, leaving an 18-inch end—16 (16, 18) sts on each needle.

Graft toe sts tog using Kitchener stitch. ●

Cozy Cabin

Design by Kim Wagner

These super stretchy socks use a fun seeded rib stitch that will hug your feet in the best way.

SKILL LEVEL

Intermediate

SIZE

Woman's medium (large); to fit shoe size 5 to 7 (8 to 10)

Instructions are given for the smaller size, with larger sizes in parentheses. When only 1 number is given, it applies to both sizes.

FINISHED MEASUREMENT

Foot Circumference: 6½ (7½) inches

Note: Sock will stretch to 8½ (9½) inches.

MATERIALS

- Expression Fiber Arts Resilient Sock (fingering weight; 100% superwash merino; 400 yds/113g per skein): 1 skein first fall hike
- Size 1 (2.5mm) double-point needles (set of 4) or size needed to obtain gauge
- Removable stitch marker

1 SUPER FINE

GAUGE

32 sts and 46 rnds = 4 inches/10cm in St st.

To save time, take time to check gauge.

OVERVIEW:

♡ Top-down construction
♡ Rib leg and instep
♡ Slip stitch heel flap
♡ Standard gusset
♡ Wedge toe
♡ Kitchener stitch

PATTERN STITCH

Note: A chart is provided for those preferring to work pat st from a chart.

Seeded Rib (multiple of 6 sts)

Rnd 1: *K2, p3, k1; rep from * around.

Rnd 2: *K1, p1; rep from * around.

Rep Rnds 1 and 2 for pat.

SEEDED RIB CHART

SOCK
Make 2.

LEG

Cast on 60 (72) sts. Divide sts evenly among 3 dpns. Pm on first st of rnd and join to work in the rnd, taking care not to twist sts.

Beg Seeded Rib; work even until piece measures 6 (7) inches or desired length for leg, ending with Rnd 2.

HEEL FLAP

Slip first 30 (36) sts onto 1 dpn for heel flap. Place rem 30 (36) sts evenly onto 2 needles for instep, removing beg-of-rnd marker.

Work back and forth in rows on 30 (36) heel sts only.

Row 1 (RS): *Sl 1 kwise, k1; rep from * to end.

Row 2 (WS): Sl 1 pwise, purl to end.

Rep [Rows 1 and 2] 13 (16) more times, then rep Row 1 once more.

Turn Heel

Row 1 (WS): P17 (20), p2tog, p1, turn.

Row 2 (RS): Sl 1 kwise, k5, k2tog, k1, turn.

Note: There is now a gap between sts at each turning point.

Row 3: Sl 1 pwise, purl to 1 st before gap, p2tog, p1, turn.

Row 4: Sl 1 kwise, knit to 1 st before turn, k2tog, k1, turn.

Rep Rows 3 and 4 until all sts have been worked, ending with Row 4—18 (20) sts.

Note: On last rep of Rows 3 and 4 for size large, omit p1 or k1 after final dec.

GUSSET

Set-up rnd: With RS of heel flap facing, with Needle 1, pick up and knit 15 (18) sts along side edge of heel flap; with Needle 2, work Rnd 1 of Seeded Rib across 30 (36) instep sts; with Needle 3, pick up and knit 15 (18) sts along opposite side edge of heel flap, then knit across first 9 (10) sts of heel. Slip rem 9 (10) sts of heel flap onto Needle 1—78 (92) sts; 24 (38) sts on Needles 1 and 3, and 30 (36) sts on Needle 2.

Note: New beg of rnd is at center of heel.

Next rnd: Needle 1: Knit to end of needle; **Needle 2:** Work Rnd 2 of Seeded Rib; **Needle 3:** Knit to end.

Dec rnd: Needle 1: Knit to last 3 sts on needle, k2tog, k1; **Needle 2:** Work in pat to end of needle; **Needle 3:** K1, ssk, knit to end—1 st dec each on Needles 1 and 3.

Rep last 2 rnds 8 (9) more times—60 (72) sts; 15 (18) sts each on Needles 1 and 3, and 30 (36) sts on Needle 2.

FOOT

Work even until foot measures 8 (8½) inches from back of heel or to approx 1½ inches less than desired length.

TOE

Rnd 1: Needle 1: Knit to last 3 sts on needle, k2tog, k1; **Needle 2:** K1, ssk, knit to last 3 sts on needle, k2tog, k1; **Needle 3:** K1, ssk, knit to end—4 sts dec.

Rnd 2: Knit.

Rep [Rnds 1 and 2] 7 (8) more times—28 (36) sts.

Next rnd: With Needle 3, knit across Needle 1—14 (18) sts on each needle.

Cut yarn, leaving a 12-inch tail.

FINISHING

Using Kitchener stitch, graft toe sts tog. Weave in all ends. ●

Lace Wedge

Design by Kim Wagner

The easy-to-work lace patterning in these socks creates a rhythmic knitting experience.

OVERVIEW:

- ♡ Top-down construction
- ♡ 1x1 rib cuff
- ♡ Lace stitch pattern on leg and instep
- ♡ Slip stitch heel flap
- ♡ Standard gusset
- ♡ Wedge toe
- ♡ Kitchener stitch

SKILL LEVEL
Intermediate

SIZE
Woman's medium; to fit shoe size 7 to 9

FINISHED MEASUREMENT
Foot Circumference: 7 inches

MATERIALS
- Lana Grossa Meilenweit Merino Hand-Dyed (fingering weight, 80% merino, 20% nylon; 375 yds/95g per hank): 1 hank Nanda #308
- Size 1 (2.25mm) double-point needles (set of 5) or size needed to obtain gauge
- Removable stitch marker

GAUGE
34 sts and 44 rnds = 4 inches/10cm in St st.

To save time, take time to check gauge.

PATTERN STITCHES

1X1 RIB (EVEN NUMBER OF STS)
Rnd 1: *K1, p1; rep from * around.

Rep Rnd 1 for pat.

LACE WEDGE (MULTIPLE OF 15 STS)
Note: A chart is provided for those preferring to work pat from a chart.

Rnd 1: *Yo, ssk, k13; rep from * around.

Rnd 2 and all even-numbered rnds: Knit around.

Rnd 3: *K1, yo, ssk, k12; rep from * around.

Rnd 5: *[Yo, ssk] twice, k11; rep from * around.

Rnd 7: *K1, [yo, ssk] twice, k10; rep from * around.

Rnd 9: *[Yo, ssk] 3 times, k9; rep from * around.

Rnd 11: *K1, [yo, ssk] 3 times, k8; rep from * around.

Rnd 13: *[Yo, ssk] 4 times, k7; rep from * around.

Rnd 15: *K1, [yo, ssk] 4 times, k6; rep from * around.

Rnd 17: *[Yo, ssk] 5 times, k5; rep from * around.

Rnd 19: *K1, [yo, ssk] 5 times, k4; rep from * around.

Rnd 21: *K13, k2tog, yo; rep from * around.

Rnd 23: *K12, k2tog, yo, k1; rep from * around.

Rnd 25: *K11, [k2tog, yo] twice; rep from * around.

Rnd 27: *K10, [k2tog, yo] twice, k1; rep from * around.

Rnd 29: *K9, [k2tog, yo] 3 times; rep from * around.

Rnd 31: *K8, [k2tog, yo] 3 times, k1; rep from * around.

Rnd 33: *K7, [k2tog, yo] 4 times; rep from * around.

Rnd 35: *K6, [k2tog, yo] 4 times, k1; rep from * around.

Rnd 37: *K5, [k2tog, yo] 5 times; rep from * around.

Rnd 39: *K4, [k2tog, yo] 5 times, k1; rep from * around.

Rnd 40: Knit around.

Rep Rnds 1–40 for pat.

STITCH KEY
- ☐ Knit
- ○ Yo
- ╲ Ssk
- ╱ K2tog

LACE WEDGE CHART

15-st rep

SOCK

Make 2.

CUFF

Loosely cast on 60 sts. Divide sts evenly among 4 dpns. Pm on first st of rnd and join to work in the rnd, taking care not to twist sts.

Beg 1x1 Rib; work 10 rnds even.

Next rnd: Knit around.

LEG

Beg Lace Wedge pat; work Rnds 1–40 once, then Rnds 1–20 once.

HEEL

Slip first 30 sts onto 1 dpn for heel flap. Place rem 30 sts onto 2 needles for instep, removing beg-of-rnd marker.

Work back and forth on 30 heel flap sts only:

Row 1 (RS): *Sl 1, k1; rep from * across.

Row 2: Sl 1, purl across.

Rows 3–28: Rep [Rows 1 and 2] 13 more times.

Row 29: Rep Row 1.

Turn Heel

Row 1 (WS): P17, p2tog, p1, turn.

Row 2: Sl 1, k5, ssk, k1, turn.

Note: There is now a gap between sts at each turning point.

Row 3: Sl 1, purl to st before gap, p2tog, p1, turn.

Row 4: Sl 1, knit to st before gap, ssk, k1, turn.

Rep Rows 3 and 4 until all sts have been worked—18 sts.

GUSSET

Set-up rnd: With RS of heel flap facing, with Needle 1, pick up and knit 15 sts along side edge of heel flap; with Needles 2 and 3, work Rnd 21 of Lace Wedge pat across instep sts; with Needle 4, pick up and knit 15 sts along side edge of heel flap, then knit across first 9 sts of heel—78 sts; 24 sts each on Needles 1 and 4, and 15 sts each on Needles 2 and 3. Pm for new beg of rnd at center of heel.

Rnd 2: Needle 1: Knit; **Needles 2 and 3:** Work Lace Wedge pat; **Needle 4:** Knit.

Rnd 3: Needle 1: Knit to last 3 sts on needle, k2tog, k1; **Needles 2 and 3:** Work in pat to end of needles; **Needle 4:** K1, ssk, knit to end—2 sts dec.

Rep [Rnds 2 and 3] 8 more times—60 sts; 15 sts each needle.

FOOT

Work even until foot measures 7½ inches from back of heel or to approx 2 inches less than desired length.

TOE

Rnd 1: Needle 1: Knit to last 3 sts on needle, k2tog, k1; **Needle 2:** K1, ssk, knit to end of needle; **Needles 3 and 4:** Rep Needles 1 and 2—4 sts dec.

Rnd 2: Knit around.

Rep [Rnds 1 and 2] 8 more times—24 sts.

Next rnd: With Needle 4, knit across Needle 1. Cut yarn, leaving a 12-inch tail.

FINISHING

Using Kitchener stitch, graft toe sts tog. Weave in all ends. ●

FIT ADJUSTMENTS:

With an allover stitch pattern, it can be difficult to work larger circumferences. For every half inch, you will need to add about 4 stitches. This is assuming your gauge matches the gauge stated in the pattern. There are 4 repeats of the stitch pattern worked to make the stated size in the pattern. You can add stitches of plain stockinette stitch between each repeat of the stitch pattern. Divide the number of stitches that you need to add by 4. Then place those stitches between each stitch pattern section. You may find that you will not be able to have an even number of stitches between each set. Just space them in a way that will be appealing to you.

You may find it helpful to mark each stitch pattern repeat with stitch markers. This will also help you with keeping track of your added stitches as they will be the short span of stitches between each set of markers.

Also keep in mind that this will change the overall look of your socks from what is pictured. So before attempting the adjustment, make sure you are okay with the change.

Summer Shorts

Design by Lena Skvagerson

Shorties make for a super quick knit. This sock is decorated with a nice eyelet pattern and a cute little pompom to top it off.

SKILL LEVEL
Easy

SIZE
Woman's small (medium, large); to fit shoe size 5 to 6 (7 to 8, 9 to 10).

Instructions are given for the smallest size, with larger sizes in parentheses. When only 1 number is given, it applies to all sizes.

FINISHED MEASUREMENT
Foot Circumference: 7¼ (7¾, 8¼) inches

MATERIALS
- Lana Grossa Meilenweit Merino Sock (fingering weight; 80% merino, 20% polyamide; 375 yds/95g per hank): 1 hank #2 amla
- Size 1½ (2.5mm) double-point needles (set of 5) or size needed to obtain gauge
- Removable stitch marker
- Stitch markers
- Stitch holder

1 SUPER FINE

GAUGE
32 sts and 40 rnds = 4 inches/10cm in St st.

To save time, take time to check gauge.

PATTERN STITCH
Eyelet [panel of 30 (32, 34) sts]
Rnd 1: K0 (1, 2), [k2tog, yo, k4] 5 times, k0 (1, 2).

Rnds 2–6: Knit.

Rnd 7: K3 (4, 5), [k2tog, yo, k4] 4 times, k2tog, yo, k1 (2, 3).

Rnds 8–12: Knit.

Rep Rnds 1–12 for pat.

OVERVIEW:
- ♡ Top-down construction
- ♡ Half twisted rib cuff
- ♡ Stockinette stitch heel flap
- ♡ Round or French heel
- ♡ Standard gusset
- ♡ Random eyelet instep
- ♡ Star toe
- ♡ Cinched toe closure

SOCK

Make 2.

LEG

Cast on 60 (64, 68) sts. Divide sts evenly among 3 dpns. Pm on first st of rnd and join to work in the rnd.

Rnd 1: *K1, p1; rep from * to end.

Rnd 2: *K1-tbl, p1; rep from * to end.

Rep Rnd 2 until piece measures approx 1 inch, or to desired length.

HEEL FLAP

Place last 30 (32, 34) sts worked onto st holder for instep. Transfer first 30 (32, 34) sts of rnd onto one needle for heel flap.

Working back and forth on heel flap sts only, work 14 (16, 18) rows in St st, beg with a knit row. On last row, pm 10 (11, 11) sts in from each edge [10 (10, 12) sts between markers in center].

SHAPE HEEL

Row 1 (RS): Sl 1 kwise, knit to 2nd marker, ssk, knit to end—1 st dec.

Row 2 (WS): Sl 1 pwise, purl to 2nd marker, p2tog, purl to end—1 st dec.

Rep [Rows 1 and 2] 9 (10, 10) times—12 (12, 14) sts rem; 1 st each side of marked center sts.

Remove markers on last row.

Next row (RS): K6 (6, 7).

GUSSET

Set-up rnd (RS): K6 (6, 7) (Needle 1), with same needle, pick up and knit 16 (18, 18) sts along side edge of heel flap; k30 (32, 34) sts from st holder onto 2nd dpn (Needle 2); with 3rd dpn (Needle 3), pick up and knit 16 (18, 18) sts along opposite side edge of heel flap, then knit rem 6 (6, 7) sts from heel flap—74 (80, 84) sts.

Note: *New beg of rnd is at center of heel.*

Rnd 1: Knit.

Rnd 2: Needle 1: Knit to last 3 sts on needle, k2tog, k1; **Needle 2:** Knit to end of needle; **Needle 3:** K1, ssk, knit to end of needle—2 sts dec.

Rnds 3–8: Rep [Rnds 1 and 2] 3 times—66 (72, 76) sts rem.

Rnd 9: Needle 1: Knit to end of needle; **Needle 2:** Work Eyelet pat to end of needle; **Needle 3:** Knit to end of needle.

Rnd 10: Needle 1: Knit to last 3 sts on needle, k2tog, k1; **Needle 2:** Work Eyelet pat to end of needle; **Needle 3:** K1, ssk, knit to end of needle—2 sts dec.

Rep [Rnds 9 and 10] 3 (4, 4) more times—58 (62, 66) sts rem; 14 (15, 16) sts on Needles 1 and 3, and 30 (32, 34) sts on Needle 2.

FOOT

Work even, knitting all sts on Needles 1 and 3 and working in Eyelet pat as established on Needle 2 until foot measures 7½ (8, 8½) inches from back of heel, or to 1½ inches shorter than desired length.

Next rnd: K2, ssk, [k27 (8, 4), ssk] 1 (5, 9) time(s), k25 (8, 8)—56 sts rem.

Knit 1 rnd.

TOE

Rnd 1: *K2tog, k5; rep from * to end—48 sts rem.

Rnds 2–4: Knit.

Rnd 5: *K2tog, k4; rep from * to end—40 sts rem.

Rnds 6–8: Knit.

Rnd 9: *K2tog, k3; rep from * to end—32 sts rem.

Rnds 10–12: Knit.

Rnd 13: *K2, k2tog; rep from * to end—24 sts rem.

Rnds 14 and 15: Knit.

Rnd 16: *K1, k2tog; rep from * to end—16 sts rem.

Rnd 17: Knit.

Rnd 18: *K2tog; rep from * to end—8 sts rem.

Cut yarn, leaving an 8-inch tail. Draw tail through rem sts and pull firmly to close.

FINISHING

Weave in all ends.

Pompom

Make 2 1-inch pompoms and attach a pompom to center of ribbing at back of each sock. ●

TIPS:

When beginning the cuff, cast on using a needle 2 to 3 sizes larger, then slip your stitches onto the correct size double-point needles when setting up to knit your first round.

To avoid color pooling, divide hank into 2 balls and alternate balls every 2 rnds/rows.

Gansey Grace

Design by Lena Skvagerson

These socks will keep your interest as you play with different knit and purl stitch patterns. Blocking will really help these socks shine.

SKILL LEVEL
Intermediate

SIZE
Woman's small/medium (medium/large); to fit shoe size 5 to 7 (8 to 10)

Instructions are given for the smallest size, with larger sizes in parentheses. When only 1 number is given, it applies to both sizes.

FINISHED MEASUREMENT
Foot Circumference: 7½ (8¾) inches

MATERIALS
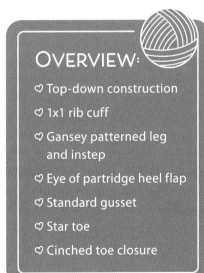

- Anzula Luxury Fibers Haiku (fingering weight; 70% merino/20% bamboo/10% nylon; 425 yds/100g per skein): 1 skein slate
- Size 1½ (2.5mm) double-point needles (set of 5) or size to obtain gauge
- Removable stitch marker
- Stitch holder

GAUGE
30 sts and 44 rows = 4 inches/10cm in St st.

To save time, take time to check gauge.

SPECIAL ABBREVIATIONS
1 over 3 Left Slipped Cross (1/3 LSC): Sl 1 kwise wyib, k1, yo, k1, pass slipped st over last 3 sts on RH needle.

Make 1 Purlwise (M1P): Insert LH needle from back to front under horizontal strand between last st worked and next st on LH needle; purl into front of resulting loop.

PATTERN STITCH
Cuff Ribbing (even number of sts)
All rnds: *K1, p1; rep from * around.

SOCK
Make 2.

CUFF
Cast on 60 (66) sts. Divide sts among 3 dpns. Pm on first st of rnd and join to work in the rnd, taking care not to twist sts.

Knit 2 rnds.

Beg Cuff Ribbing; work 14 (18) rnds even.

LEG
Rnd 1: Knit.

Rnds 2 and 3: Purl.

Rnd 4: Knit.

Rnds 5–7: *K3, p3; rep from * around.

Rnds 8–10: *P3, k3; rep from * around.

Rnds 11–22: Rep Rnds 5–10 twice.

Rnd 23: Knit.

Rnds 24 and 25: Purl.

Rnd 26: Knit.

Rnd 27: *P1, k1; rep from * around.

Rnd 28: Knit.

Rnds 29–40: Rep [Rnds 27 and 28] 6 times.

Rnds 41 and 42: Purl.

Rnds 43–45: Knit.

Rnd 46: *P1, k5; rep from * around.

Rnd 47: *K1, p1, k3, p1; rep from * around.

Rnd 48: *P1, k1; rep from * around.

Rnd 49: *K1, p1; rep from * around.

Rnd 50: *K2, [p1, k1] twice; rep from * around.

Rnd 51: *K3, p1, k2; rep from * around.

Rnds 52–54: Knit.

Rnds 55 and 56: Purl.

OVERVIEW:
- ♡ Top-down construction
- ♡ 1x1 rib cuff
- ♡ Gansey patterned leg and instep
- ♡ Eye of partridge heel flap
- ♡ Standard gusset
- ♡ Star toe
- ♡ Cinched toe closure

HEEL FLAP

Sl last 30 sts of rnd onto 1 dpn for heel flap. Place rem 30 (36) sts on st holder for instep, removing beg-of-rnd marker.

Work back and forth in rows on 30 heel sts only.

Row 1 (WS): Sl 1, purl to end.

Row 2 (RS): *Sl 1, k1; rep from * to end.

Row 3: Sl 1, purl to end.

Row 4: Sl 2, *k1, sl 1; rep from * to last 2 sts, k2.

Rep Rows 1–4 until heel measures 2¼ (2½) inches, ending with a WS row.

Turn Heel

Row 1 (RS): K17, ssk, k1, turn.

Row 2 (WS): Sl 1, p5, p2tog, p1, turn.

Note: *There is now a gap between sts at each turning point.*

Row 3: Sl 1, knit to 1 st before gap, ssk, k1, turn.

Row 4: Sl 1, purl to 1 st before gap, p2tog, p1, turn.

Rep Rows 3 and 4 until all sts have been worked, ending with Row 4—18 sts.

GUSSET

Set-up rnd: With RS of heel flap facing, knit across first 9 sts on heel flap, with another dpn (Needle 1), knit the next 9 sts on heel flap, with same needle, pick up and knit 16 (17) sts along side edge of heel flap; with Needle 2, knit 30 (36) sts of instep; with Needle 3, pick up and knit 16 (17) sts along opposite side edge of heel flap, then knit across rem 9 sts on heel flap—80 (88) sts; 25 (26) sts each on Needles 1 and 3, and 30 (36) sts on Needle 2.

Note: *New beg of rnd is at center of heel.*

Knit 1 rnd.

Rnd 1: Needle 1: Knit to last 3 sts on needle, k2tog, k1; **Needle 2:** *K1, p1; rep from * to end of needle; **Needle 3:** K1, ssk, knit to end—1 st dec each on Needles 1 and 3.

Rnd 2: Needle 1: Knit; **Needle 2:** *K1, p1; rep from * to end of needle; **Needle 3:** Knit.

Rnd 3: Needle 1: Knit to last 3 sts on needle, k2tog, k1; **Needle 2:** *P1, k1; rep from * to end of needle; **Needle 3:** K1, ssk, knit to end—1 st dec each on Needles 1 and 3.

Rnd 4: Needle 1: Knit; **Needle 2:** *P1, k1; rep from * to end of needle; **Needle 3:** Knit.

Rnds 5–16: Rep [Rnds 1–4] 3 times—64 (72) sts; 17 (18) sts each on Needles 1 and 3, and 30 (36) sts on Needle 2.

Rnd 17: Needle 1: Knit to last 3 sts on needle, k2tog, k1; **Needle 2:** Knit; **Needle 3:** K1, ssk, knit—1 st dec each on Needles 1 and 3.

Rnd 18: Knit.

Rnd 19: Needle 1: Knit to last 3 sts on needle, k2tog, k1; **Needle 2:** Purl; **Needle 3:** K1, ssk, knit—1 st dec each on Needles 1 and 3—60 (68) sts; 15 (16) sts each on Needles 1 and 3, and 30 (36) sts on Needle.

Rnd 20: Needle 1: Knit; **Needle 2:** Purl; **Needle 3:** Knit.

Rnd 21: Rep Rnd 17—58 (66) sts; 14 (15) sts each on Needles 1 and 3, and 30 (36) sts on Needle 2.

FOOT

Size Small/Medium Only

Rnd 1: Needle 1: Knit; **Needle 2:** P3, *k3, p4; rep from * to last 6 sts, k3, p3; **Needle 3:** Knit.

Size Medium/Large Only

Rnd 1: Needle 1: Knit; **Needle 2:** P3, *k3, p4; rep from * to last 5 sts, k3, M1P, p2; **Needle 3:** Knit—67 sts; 15 sts each on Needles 1 and 3, and 37 sts on Needle 2.

Both Sizes

Rnd 2: Needle 1: Knit; **Needle 2:** P3, *k3, p4; rep from * to last 6 sts, k3, p3; **Needle 3:** Knit.

Rnd 3: Needle 1: Knit; **Needle 2:** P3, *1/3 LSC, p4; rep from * to last 6 sts, 1/3 LSC, p3; **Needle 3:** Knit.

Rnds 4 and 5: Rep Rnd 2.

Rnds 6–13: Rep Rnds 2–5 twice.

Size Small/Medium Only

Rnd 14: Knit.

Size Medium/Large Only

Rnd 14: Needle 1: Knit; **Needle 2:** Knit to last 2 sts, k2tog; **Needle 3:** Knit—66 sts; 15 sts each on Needles 1 and 3, and 36 sts on Needle 2.

Both Sizes

Rnds 15 and 16: Needle 1: Knit; **Needle 2:** Purl; **Needle 3:** Knit.

Rnd 17: Knit.

Rnd 18: Needle 1: Knit; **Needle 2:** *K5, p1; rep from * to end of needle; **Needle 3:** Knit.

Rnd 19: Needle 1: Knit; Needle 2: *P1, k5; rep from * to end of needle; **Needle 3:** Knit.

Rnd 20: Needle 1: Knit; **Needle 2:** *K1, p1, k4; rep from * to end of needle; **Needle 3:** Knit.

Rnd 21: Needle 1: Knit; **Needle 2:** *K2, p1, k3; rep from * to end of needle; **Needle 3:** Knit.

Rnd 22: Needle 1: Knit; **Needle 2:** *K3, p1, k2; rep from * to end of needle; **Needle 3:** Knit.

Rnd 23: Needle 1: Knit; **Needle 2:** *K4, p1, k1; rep from * to end of needle; **Needle 3:** Knit.

Rnds 24–29 (35): Rep Rnds 18–23 once (twice).

Rnd 30 (36): Rep Rnd 18.

Rnd 31 (37): Knit.

Rnds 32 and 33 (38 and 39): Rep Rnds 15 and 16.

Rnd 34 (40): Knit.

Rep last rnd until foot measures approx 7½ (8) inches from back of heel, or to 1¾ (2) inches shorter than desired length.

TOE

Next rnd: Needle 1: Knit; **Needle 2:** Ssk, knit to last 2 sts, ssk; **Needle 3:** Knit—56 (64) sts; 14 (15) sts each on Needles 1 and 3, and 28 (34) sts on Needle 2.

Next rnd: Knit.

Size Medium/Large Only

Next rnd: *K2tog, k6; rep from * around—56 sts.

Next rnd: Knit.

Both Sizes

Rnd 1: *K2tog, k5; rep from * around—48 sts.

Rnds 2–4: Knit.

Rnd 5: *K2tog, k4; rep from * around—40 sts.

Rnds 6–8: Knit.

Rnd 9: *K2tog, k3; rep from * around—32 sts.

Rnds 10–12: Knit.

Rnd 13: *K2, k2tog; rep from * around—24 sts.

Rnds 14 and 15: Knit.

Rnd 16: *K1, k2tog; rep from * around—16 sts.

Rnd 17: Knit.

Rnd 18: *K2tog; rep from * around—8 sts.

Cut yarn, leaving an 8-inch tail. Draw tail through rem sts and pull firmly to close.

FINISHING

Weave in all ends. Block to even out texture. ●

A Few Uses For Stitch Markers:

There are many uses for stitch markers. They are used to mark the beginning of the round. They can also be used, in a sock like this, to denote each separate stitch pattern. In the leg of this sock, there is lacework, faux cables on each side of the lace and ribbing on the back. Separate each section by stitch markers to make them easy to identify. When using many stitch markers in a round like this, just make sure that your beginning-of-round marker is unique.

Stitch markers can also be used to track your rounds. Place a stitch marker every 10 rounds (or your preferred distance). This will help you easily make sure your second sock has the same number of rounds as the first sock. You can easily see and count the markers vertically along your sock.

Mermaid Lace

Design by Britt Schmiesing

Try your hand at toe-up socks that feature a beautiful lace pattern and a short-row heel.

SKILL LEVEL
Intermediate

SIZE
Woman's small (medium, large); to fit shoe size 5 to 6 (7 to 8, 9 to 10)

Instructions are given for the smallest size, with larger sizes in parentheses. When only 1 number is given, it applies to all sizes.

FINISHED MEASUREMENT
Foot Circumference: 7 (8, 9) inches

MATERIALS
- SweetGeorgia Yarns Tough Love Sock (fingering weight; 80% superwash merino/20% nylon; 425 yds/115g per skein): 1 skein peachy

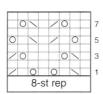

- Size 1 (2.25mm) double-point needles (set of 5) or size needed to obtain gauge
- Removable stitch markers

GAUGE
38 sts and 52 rows = 4 inches/10cm in St st.

To save time, take time to check gauge.

SPECIAL ABBREVIATION
Double stitch (DS): On WS rows: Slip st pwise to RH needle wyif. Bring yarn up and over the RH needle to RS of work, then back to WS between needles. 2 legs will be visible on RH needle; treat them as 1 st. **On RS rows:** Slip st pwise to RH needle wyif. Bring yarn up and over RH needle to back of work. 2 legs are twisted around each other; treat them as 1 st. To close DS, knit both legs of DS tog.

PATTERN STITCHES
Lace (multiple of 8 sts)
Note: A chart is provided for those preferring to work pat st from a chart.

Rnd 1: *K1, ssk, k1, [yo, k1] twice, k2tog; rep from * to end.

Rnd 2 and all even-numbered rnds: Knit.

Rnd 3: *K1, ssk, yo, k3, yo, k2tog; rep from * to end.

Rnd 5: *K1, yo, k1, k2tog, k1, ssk, k1, yo; rep from * to end.

Rnd 7: *K2, yo, k2tog, k1, ssk, yo, k1; rep from * to end.

Rnd 8: Knit.

Rep Rnds 1–8 for pat.

STITCH KEY
- ☐ K
- ⦾ Yo
- ╱ K2tog
- ╲ Ssk

LACE CHART

Half Twisted Rib
All rnds: *K1-tbl, p1; rep from * around.

OVERVIEW:
- ♡ Toe-up construction
- ♡ Turkish cast-on
- ♡ Rounded wedge toe
- ♡ Lace instep and leg
- ♡ German short-row heel
- ♡ Half twisted rib cuff
- ♡ Sewn bind-off

SOCK
Make 2.

TOE
Using 2 dpns held tog and Turkish cast-on, cast on 8 (12, 16) sts.

Rnd 1: *K1 (2, 3), kfb, pm; rep from * around. Pm on first st of rnd—12 (16, 20) sts.

Rnd 2: *Knit to 1 st before marker, kfb sm; rep from * around—4 sts inc.

Divide sts evenly onto 4 dpns.

Rnds 3–8: Rep [Rnd 2] 6 more times—40 (44, 48) sts.

Rnd 9 and all odd-numbered rnds: Knit.

Rnd 10: *K7 (7, 8), p1, knit to 1 st before marker, kfb; rep from * around—44 (48, 52) sts.

Rnd 12: *K6 (6, 7), p1, knit to 1 st before marker, kfb; rep from * around—48 (52, 56) sts.

Rnd 14: *K5 (5, 6), p1, knit to 1 st before marker, kfb; rep from * around—52 (56, 60) sts.

Rnd 16: *K4 (4, 5), p1, knit to 1 st before marker, kfb; rep from * around—56 (60, 64) sts.

Rnd 18: *K3 (3, 4), p1, knit to 1 st before marker, kfb; rep from * around—60 (64, 68) sts.

Rnd 20: *K2 (2, 3), p1, knit to 1 st before marker, kfb; rep from * around—64 (68, 72) sts.

Size Small Only
Rnd 22: *K1, p1, knit to marker; rep from * around.

Sizes Medium & Large Only
Rnd 22: *K – (1, 2), p1, knit to 1 st before marker, kfb; rep from * around—(72, 76) sts.

Size Large Only
Rnd 24: *K1, p1, knit to 1 st before marker, kfb; rep from * around—80 sts.

All Sizes
Knit 1 rnd.

FOOT
Next rnd: Work Lace pat over first 32 (32, 40) sts for instep, knit to end.

Rep last rnd until foot measures 6½ (7½, 8¼) inches from tip of toe or 1½ (1¾, 2) inches shorter than desired length to back of heel.

GERMAN SHORT-ROW HEEL
First Half
Turn work so WS is facing.

Short row 1 (WS): DS, p31 (39, 39) (working these sts onto 1 needle), turn, leaving rem 32 (32, 40) sts on 2 needles for instep.

Short row 2 (RS): Working on sole sts only, DS, knit to DS, turn.

Short row 3: DS, purl to DS, turn.

Rep [Short rows 2 and 3] 8 (11, 11) more times, then rep Short row 2 once—10 (13, 13) DSs each side of center 12 (14, 14) sts.

Next rnd: Knit to end of sole sts (closing DSs as you come to them), work in pat across instep sts.

2nd Half
Short row 1 (RS): K22 (27, 27) (closing rem DSs as you come to them), k1, turn.

Short row 2 (WS): DS, p13 (15, 15), turn.

Short row 3: DS, knit to DS from previous RS row, close DS, k1, turn.

Short row 4: DS, purl to DS from previous WS row, close DS, p1, turn.

Rep Short rows 3 and 4 until all sts have been worked across, ending with Short row 4.

Short row 5: DS, knit across sole sts, closing DS.

Next rnd: Work Lace pat across instep sts, M1R, knit to end of sole sts, M1L—66 (74, 82) sts.

Next rnd: Work Lace pat across instep sts, k2tog, knit to last 2 sole sts, ssk—64 (72, 80) sts.

Redistribute sts if necessary so there are 16 (16, 20) sts each on Needles 1 and 2 for instep, and 16 (16, 20) sts each on Needles 3 and 4 for sole. Pm on first st on Needle 1 for beg of rnd.

LEG
Work in Lace pat as established across all sts (closing rem DSs on first rnd) for 5½ (6, 6½) inches or 1 inch shorter than desired leg length, ending Lace pat with Rnd 4 or 8.

CUFF
Work Half Twisted Rib pat until cuff measures approx 1 inch.

Cut yarn, leaving a tail 3 to 4 times the circumference of the cuff. Thread tail on tapestry needle. Bind off all sts as follows:

Step 1: Insert tapestry needle through first st as if to purl, leaving st on LH needle.

Step 2: Going between the first and 2nd sts on LH needle, insert tapestry needle into 2nd st as if to knit, leaving st on LH needle.

Step 3: Insert tapestry needle into first knit st as if to knit, dropping st from LH needle; insert tapestry needle in to next knit st as if to purl, leaving st on LH needle. Pull yarn snug.

Step 4: Insert tapestry needle into first purl st as if to purl, dropping st from LH needle; going behind next st, insert tapestry needle into next purl st as if to knit, leaving st on LH needle. Pull yarn snug.

Rep Steps 3 and 4 until until 2 sts rem.

Step 5: Insert tapestry needle into first st as if to knit, dropping st from LH needle; insert tapestry needle into first st of next rnd (first bound-off st) as if to knit.

Step 6: Insert tapestry needle into rem purl st as if to purl, dropping st from LH needle; insert tapestry needle into left leg of first st of next rnd; insert tapestry needle through to back of work to weave in.

FINISHING
Weave in all ends. ●

> **TIP:**
> The Lace pattern is quite stretchy. If you find you are between sizes, choosing the smaller size will open the pattern up more.

Lavender Lace

Design by Lena Skvagerson

You really get to play with techniques and stitch patterns in these lovely socks.

SKILL LEVEL
Intermediate

SIZE
Woman's small (medium, large); to fit shoe size 5 to 6 (7 to 8, 9 to 10).

Instructions are given for the smallest size, with larger sizes in parentheses. When only 1 number is given, it applies to all sizes.

FINISHED MEASUREMENT
Foot Circumference: 7 (7½, 8) inches

MATERIALS
- Expression Fiber Arts Resilient Sock (fingering weight; 100% superwash merino wool; 400 yds/113g per skein): 1 skein lavender ice cream
- Size 1½ (2.5mm) double-point needles (set of 5) or size needed to obtain gauge
- Removable stitch marker
- Stitch holder

GAUGE
34 sts and 44 rows = 4 inches/10cm in St st.

To save time, take time to check gauge.

SPECIAL ABBREVIATIONS
Centered Double Decrease (CDD): Sl 2 sts as if to k2tog, k1, p2sso to dec 2 sts.

Left slipped cross (LSC): Slip the next st kwise wyib, k2, pass the slipped st over the k2—1 st dec.

PATTERN STITCH
Lace [panel of 31 (33, 35) sts at beg and end; st count varies]

Rnd 1: P1, LSC, p1 (2, 2), k21 (21, 23), p1 (2, 2), LSC, p1—29 (31, 33) sts.

Rnd 2: P1, k1, yo, k1, p1 (2, 2), k1 (1, 2), [k1, yo, ssk, k1, k2tog, yo] 3 times, k2 (2, 3), p1 (2, 2), k1, yo, k1, p1—31 (33, 35) sts.

Rnd 3: P1, k3, p1 (2, 2), k21 (21, 23), p1 (2, 2), k3, p1.

Rnd 4: P1, k3, p1 (2, 2), k3 (3, 4), [yo, k3] 6 times, k0 (0, 1), p1 (2, 2), k3, p1—37 (39, 41) sts.

Rnd 5: P1, LSC, p1 (2, 2), k27 (27, 29), p1 (2, 2), LSC, p1—35 (37, 39) sts.

Rnd 6: P1, k1, yo, k1, p1 (2, 2), k1 (1, 2), k2tog, [yo, ssk, k1, k2tog, yo, CDD] twice, yo, ssk, k1, k2tog, yo, ssk, k1 (1, 2), p1 (2, 2), k1, yo, k1, p1—31 (33, 35) sts.

Rnd 7: P1, k3, p1 (2, 2), k21 (21, 23), p1 (2, 2), k3, p1.

Rnd 8: P1, k3, p1 (2, 2), k1 (1, 2), [k1, k2tog, yo, k1, yo, ssk] 3 times, k2 (2, 3), p1 (2, 2), k3, p1.

Rnd 9: P1, LSC, p1 (2, 2), k21 (21, 23), p1 (2, 2), LSC, p1—29 (31, 33) sts.

Rnd 10: P1, k1, yo, k1, p1 (2, 2), k3 (3, 4), [yo, k3] 6 times, k0 (0, 1), p1 (2, 2), k1, yo, k1, p1—37 (39, 41) sts.

Rnd 11: P1, k3, p1 (2, 2), k27 (27, 29), p1 (2, 2), k3, p1.

Rnd 12: P1, k3, p1 (2, 2), k1 (1, 2) *k1, k2tog, yo, CDD, yo, ssk; rep from * 3 times, k2 (2, 3), p1 (2, 2), k3, p1—31 (33, 35) sts.

Rep Rnds 1–12 for pat.

SOCK
Make 2.

CUFF
Using backward loop cast-on, loosely cast on 60 (64, 68) sts. Divide sts evenly among 4 dpns. Pm on first st of rnd and join to work in the rnd.

OVERVIEW:
- ♡ Top-down construction
- ♡ Backward loop cast-on
- ♡ Folded picot cuff
- ♡ Lace, faux cable and 1x1 rib leg
- ♡ 1x1 rib heel flap
- ♡ Standard gusset
- ♡ Rounded wedge toe
- ♡ Cinched toe closure

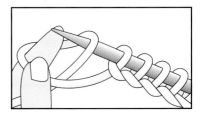

Backward Loop Cast-On

Work 7 rnds in St st (knit every rnd).

Eyelet rnd: *Yo, k2tog; rep from * to end.

Work 7 rnds in St st.

Joining rnd: Fold cast-on edge to WS with sts on cast-on rnd parallel to sts on needles, knit first st on needle tog with first cast-on st, *knit next st on needle tog with next cast-on st; rep from * to end.

Knit 1 rnd, purl 1 rnd, knit 1 rnd.

Eyelet rnd: *Yo, k2tog; rep from * to end.

Knit 1 rnd, purl 1 rnd, knit 2 rnds.

LEG

Rnds 1–48: Work Lace pat over first 31 (33, 35) sts, p1, *k1, p1; rep from * to end.

HEEL FLAP

Sl last 29 (31, 33) sts of rnd onto 1 dpn for heel flap. Place rem 31 (33, 35) sts on st holder for instep, removing beg-of-rnd marker.

Work back and forth in rows on 29 (31, 33) heel sts only.

Row 1 (WS): Sl 1, *p1, k1; rep from * to end.

Row 2 (RS): Sl 1, *k1, p1; rep from * to end.

Rep Rows 1 and 2 until heel measures 2 (2¼, 2½) inches, ending with a WS row.

Turn Heel

Row 1 (RS): K16 (17, 18), ssk, k1, turn.

Row 2 (WS): Sl 1, p4, p2tog, p1, turn.

Note: *There is now a gap between sts at each turning point.*

Row 3: Sl 1, knit to 1 st before gap, ssk, k1, turn.

Row 4: Sl 1, purl to 1 st before gap, p2tog, p1, turn.

Rep Rows 3 and 4 until all sts have been worked, ending with Row 4—17 (17, 19) sts.

Note: *For size medium, you will not have enough sts to work final p1 and k1 at end of last rep of Rows 3 and 4.*

GUSSET

Rnd 1 (RS): With RS of heel flap facing, knit across first 8 (8, 9) sts on heel flap, with another dpn (Needle 1), knit the next 9 (9, 10) sts on heel flap, with same needle, pick up and knit 16 (17, 17) sts along side edge of heel; with Needle 2, work Rnd 1 of Lace pat over 31 (33, 35) sts of instep; with Needle 3, pick up and knit 16 (17, 17) sts along opposite side edge of heel flap, then knit across rem 8 (8, 9) sts on heel flap—78 (82, 86) sts; 25 (26, 27) sts on Needle 1, 29 (31, 33) sts on Needle 2 and 24 (25, 26) sts on Needle 3.

Rnd 2: Needle 1: Knit to last st on needle, p1; **Needle 2:** Work next rnd of Lace pat; **Needle 3:** P1, knit to end—80 (84, 88) sts.

Rnd 3: Needle 1: Knit to last 3 sts on needle, k2tog, p1; **Needle 2:** Work next rnd of Lace pat; **Needle 3:** P1, ssk, knit to end—1 st dec each on Needles 1 and 3.

Rnds 4–21: Rep [Rnds 2 and 3] 9 more times, at the same time continuing with Lace pat on Needle 2, ending with Rnd 9 of Lace pat—58 (62, 66) sts; 15 (16, 17) sts on Needle 1, 29 (31, 33) sts on Needle 2 and 14 (15, 16) sts on Needle 3.

FOOT

Work even until foot measures 7 (7½, 8) inches from back of heel, or to 2 inches shorter than desired length, ending with Rnd 1 or 9 of Lace pat—58 (62, 66) sts.

TOE

Rnd 1: Needle 1: Knit to last 3 sts, k2tog, k1; **Needle 2:** K1, ssk, knit to last 3 sts, k2tog, k1; **Needle 3:** K1, ssk, knit to end—4 sts dec.

Rnds 2–4: Knit.

Rnd 5: Rep Rnd 1—50 (54, 58) sts.

Rnds 6 and 7: Knit.

Rnds 8–10: Rep Rnds 5–7—46 (50, 54) sts.

Rnd 11: Rep Rnd 1—42 (46, 50) sts.

Rnd 12: Knit.

Rnds 13–16: Rep Rnds 11 and 12—34 (38, 42) sts.

Rep [Rnd 1] 6 (7, 8) times—10 sts.

Cut yarn, leaving a 6-inch tail. Thread tail through rem sts and pull tight to close.

FINISHING

Weave in all ends. ●

> TIP:
>
> Stitch markers are going to come in handy for tracking your stitches in this pattern. Use them liberally to denote each section of the pattern stitches in each round.

Zany Zigzag

Design by Sarah Wilson

Working the zigzag completely in stockinette stitch makes this a quicker knit, and the fun zigzag is carried down through the heel.

SKILL LEVEL

Intermediate

SIZE

Woman's medium, to fit shoe size 6 to 9

FINISHED MEASUREMENT

Foot Circumference: 7¾ inches

MATERIALS

- Expression Fiber Arts Resilient Sock (fingering weight; 100% superwash merino wool; 400 yds/4 oz per skein): 1 skein first fall hike
- Size 1 (2.5mm) double-pointed needles (set of 4) or size needed to obtain gauge
- Removable stitch marker

OVERVIEW:

- ♡ Top-down construction
- ♡ Wide rib cuff
- ♡ Raised stockinette all over pattern on leg and instep
- ♡ Raised stockinette pattern heel flap
- ♡ Standard gusset
- ♡ Wedge toe
- ♡ Kitchener stitch

GAUGE

34 sts and 52 rnds = 4 inches/10cm in St st.

To save time, take time to check gauge.

SPECIAL ABBREVIATION

Right Lifted Increase (RLI): Knit into top of st (the purl bump) in the row below next st on LH needle.

PATTERN STITCHES

Cuff Rib (multiple of 11 sts)

Rnd 1: *K4, p2, k3, p2; rep from * around.

Rep Rnd 1 for pat.

Zigzag (multiple of 11 sts)

Note: A chart is provided for those preferring to work pat st from a chart.

Rnd 1: *RLI, k3, ssk, k6; rep from * around.

Rnd 2 and all even-numbered rnds: Knit.

Rnd 3: *K1, RLI, k3, ssk, k5; rep from * around.

Rnd 5: *K2, RLI, k3, ssk, k4; rep from * around.

Rnd 7: *K3, RLI, k3, ssk, k3; rep from * around.

Rnd 9: *K4, RLI, k3, ssk, k2; rep from * around.

Rnd 11: *K5, RLI, k3, ssk, k1; rep from * around.

Rnd 13: *K6, RLI, k3, ssk; rep from * around.

Rnd 15: *K6, k2tog, k3, RLI; rep from * around.

Rnd 17: *K5, k2tog, k3, RLI, k1; rep from * around.

Rnd 19: *K4, k2tog, k3, RLI, k2; rep from * around.

Rnd 21: *K3, k2tog, k3, RLI, k3; rep from * around.

Rnd 23: *K2, *k2tog, k3, RLI, k4; rep from * around.

Rnd 25: *K1, *k2tog, k3, RLI, k5; rep from * around.

Rnd 27: *K2tog, k3, RLI, k6; rep from * around.

Rnd 28: Knit.

Rep Rnds 1–28 for pat.

STITCH KEY

- ☐ K
- ☑ RLI
- ☑ K2tog
- ◩ Ssk

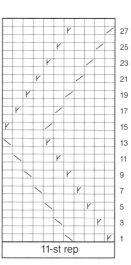

11-st rep

ZIGZAG CHART

SOCK

Make 2.

CUFF

Cast on 66 sts. Divide sts among 3 dpns as follows: **Needle 1:** 14 sts; **Needle 2:** 33 sts; **Needle 3:** 19 sts. Pm on first st of rnd and join to work in the rnd, taking care not to twist sts.

Beg Cuff Rib; work 12 rnds even.

Beg Zigzag; work Rnds 1–28 once, then Rnds 1–27 once.

HEEL FLAP

Set-up row: K22, knitting all sts onto Needle 1; k33, knitting all sts onto Needle 2 for heel flap; leave rem 11 sts on Needle 3.

Leaving instep sts on hold on Needles 1 and 3, work back and forth in established pat on 33 heel flap sts for 2 inches, purling all WS rows, and ending with a WS row.

Turn Heel

Row 1 (RS): K19, ssk, k1, turn.

Row 2 (WS): Sl 1, p6, p2tog, p1, turn.

Note: There is now a gap at each turning point.

Row 3: Sl 1, knit to 1 st before gap, ssk, k1, turn.

Row 4: Sl 1, purl to 1 st before gap, p2tog, p1, turn.

Rep Rows 3 and 4 until all sts have been worked—19 sts.

Note: On last rep of Rows 3 and 4, omit p1 or k1 after final dec.

GUSSET

Note: Needle numbers will be reassigned as you work Set-up rnd.

Set-up rnd: With Needle 1 (formerly Needle 2), knit across heel sts, pick up and knit 14 sts along edge of heel flap, and 1 st between top of heel flap and instep sts; with Needle 2 (formerly Needle 3), work established Zigzag pat across 33 instep sts; with Needle 3 (formerly Needle 1), pick up and knit 1 st between instep sts and top of heel flap, and 14 sts along edge of heel flap, knit 9 heel flap sts from new Needle 1—82 sts; 24 sts on Needle 1, 33 sts on Needle 2 and 25 sts on Needle 3.

Note: New beg of rnd is at center of heel.

Next rnd: Needle 1: Knit to end of needle; **Needle 2:** Work in pat to end of needle; **Needle 3:** Knit to end.

Next rnd: Needle 1: Knit to last 2 sts on needle, k2tog; **Needle 2:** Work in pat to end of needle; **Needle 3:** Ssk, knit to end—1 st dec each on Needles 1 and 3.

Rep last 2 rnds 7 more times—66 sts; 16 sts on Needle 1, 33 sts on Needle 2 and 17 sts on Needle 3.

FOOT

Work even until foot measures 7½ inches from back of heel or to approx 1½ inches less than desired length.

TOE

Rnd 1: Knit.

Rnd 2: Needle 1: Knit to last 3 sts on needle, k2tog, k1; **Needle 2:** K1, ssk, knit to last 3 sts on needle, k2tog, k1; **Needle 3:** K1, ssk, knit to end—4 sts dec.

Rep [Rnds 1 and 2] 9 more times—26 sts.

Next rnd: With Needle 3, knit across Needle 1—13 sts on each needle.

Cut yarn, leaving a 16-inch tail.

FINISHING

Using Kitchener stitch, graft toe sts tog. Weave in all ends. ●

FIT ADJUSTMENTS:

With an allover stitch pattern, it can be difficult to work larger circumferences. For every half inch, you will need to add about 4 stitches. This is assuming your gauge matches the gauge stated in the pattern. There are 6 repeats of the stitch pattern worked to make the stated size in the pattern. You can add stitches of plain stockinette stitch between each repeat of the stitch pattern. Divide the number of stitches that you need to add by 6. Then place those stitches between each stitch pattern section. You may find that you will not be able to have an even number of stitches between each set. Just space them in a way that will be appealing to you.

You may find it helpful to mark each stitch pattern repeat with stitch markers. This will also help you with keeping track of your added stitches as they will be the short span of stitches between each set of markers.

Midnight Blues

Design by Lena Skvagerson

Practice cabling in this pair of socks that are
sure to be a stable piece in your sock drawer.

SKILL LEVEL
Intermediate

SIZE
Woman's small/medium (large/X-large); to fit shoe size 5 to 8 (9 to 11).

Instructions are given for the smallest size, with larger size in parentheses. When only 1 number is given, it applies to both sizes.

FINISHED MEASUREMENT
Foot Circumference: 7 (7½) inches

MATERIALS
- Zen Yarn Garden super fine (fingering weight; 90% superwash merino/ 10% nylon; 400 yds/100g per skein): 1 skein midnight blue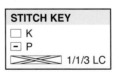
- Size 1½ (2.5mm) double-point needles (set of 4) or size needed obtain gauge
- Removable stitch marker
- 2 cable needles
- Stitch holder

GAUGE
32 sts and 44 rows = 4 inches/10cm in St st.

To save time, take time to check gauge.

SPECIAL ABBREVIATIONS
1 over 1 over 3 Left Cross (1/1/3 LC): Sl 1 st to cn and hold in front; sl next 3 sts to 2nd cn and hold in back; k1, k3 from back cn, k1 from front cn.

Make 1 Purlwise (M1P): Insert LH needle from back to front under horizontal strand between last st worked and next st on LH needle; purl into front of resulting loop.

PATTERN STITCHES
Rib (multiple of 7 sts)
All rnds: *P1, k2, p1, k2, p1; rep from * around.

Cable (multiple of 14 sts)
Note: A chart is provided for those preferring to work pat st from a chart.

Rnd 1: *P1, 1/1/3 LC, p2, k5, p1; rep from * around.

Rnds 2–4: *P1, k5, p1; rep from * around.

Rnd 5: *P1, k5, p2, 1/1/3 LC, p1; rep from * around.

Rnds 6–12: *P1, k5, p1; rep from * around.

Rnd 13: *P1, k5, p2, 1/1/3 LC, p1; rep from * around.

Rnds 14–16: *P1, k5, p1; rep from * around.

Rnd 17: *P1, 1/1/3 LC, p2, k5, p1; rep from * around.

Rnds 18–24: *P1, k5, p1; rep from * around.

Rep Rnds 1–24 for pat.

STITCH KEY	
☐	K
⊟	P
⟩⟨	1/1/3 LC

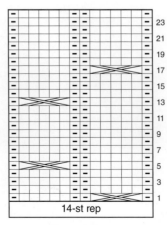

CABLE CHART

OVERVIEW:
- ♡ Top-down construction
- ♡ 1x2 rib cuff
- ♡ Cable leg and instep
- ♡ Slip stitch heel flap
- ♡ Standard gusset
- ♡ Wedge toe
- ♡ Kitchener stitch

SOCK
Make 2.

CUFF
Cast on 70 sts. Divide sts among 3 dpns. Pm on first st of rnd and join to work in the rnd.

Beg Rib pat; work 6 (8) rnds even.

LEG
Beg Cable pat; work Rnds 1–24 twice, then work Rnds 1–10 once.

HEEL FLAP
Sl last 35 sts of rnd onto 1 dpn for heel flap.

Place rem 35 sts onto st holder for instep.

Work back and forth in rows on heel sts only.

Row 1 (WS): Sl 1, purl to end.

Row 2 (RS): Sl 1, *k1, sl 1; rep from * to last 2 sts, k2.

Rep [Rows 1 and 2] 14 (16) more times.

TURN HEEL
Row 1 (WS): Sl 1, p19, p2tog, p1, turn.

Row 2 (RS): Sl 1, k6, ssk, k1, turn.

Note: There is now a gap between sts at each turning point.

Row 3: Sl 1, purl to 1 st before gap, p2tog, p1, turn.

Row 4: Sl 1, knit to 1 st before gap, ssk, k1, turn.

Rep Rows 3 and 4 until all sts have been worked, ending with a RS row—21 sts.

GUSSET

Set-up rnd: With RS of heel flap facing, using heel needle (Needle 1), pick up and knit 15 (17) sts along side edge of heel flap; with Needle 2, M1P, work 35 sts in Cable pat as established from holder for instep, M1P; with Needle 3, pick up and knit 15 (17) sts along opposite side edge of heel flap, then knit 10 heel flap sts onto same needle—88 (92) sts; 26 (28) sts on Needle 1, 37 sts on Needle 2, and 25 (27) sts on Needle 3. Rejoin to work in the rnd; pm on the first st on Needle 1 for new beg of rnd.

Rnd 1: Needle 1: Knit; **Needle 2:** P1, work in Cable pat as established to last st on needle, p1; **Needle 3:** Knit.

Rnd 2: Needle 1: Knit to last 3 sts on needle, k2tog, k1; **Needle 2:** P1, work in Cable pat as established to last st on needle, p1; **Needle 3:** K1, ssk, knit to end—2 sts dec.

Rep [Rnds 1 and 2] 10 more times—66 (70) sts; 15 (17) sts on Needle 1, 37 sts on Needle 2, and 14 (16) sts on Needle 3.

FOOT

Work even until foot measures 7 (8) inches from back of heel or to approx 2 inches shorter than desired length. Discontinue Cable pat and work in St st across all sts.

TOE

Set-up rnd: Needle 1: Knit to last 3 sts on needle, k2tog, k1; **Needle 2:** P2, [k5, p2tog] 5 times; **Needle 3:** Knit—60 (64) sts; 14 (16) sts on Needle 1, 32 sts on Needle 2, and 14 (16) sts on Needle 3.

Rnd 1: Needle 1: Knit to last 3 sts on needle, k2tog, k1; **Needle 2:** K1, ssk, knit to last 3 sts on needle, k2tog, k1; **Needle 3:** K1, ssk, knit to end—4 sts dec.

Rnd 2: Knit.

Rep [Rnds 1 and 2] 10 more times, then rep Rnd 1 once—12 (16) sts.

With Needle 3, knit to end of Needle 1; rearrange sts if necessary so that you have the same number of sts on instep and sole needles.

Cut yarn, leaving an 18-inch tail.

FINISHING

Using Kitchener stitch, graft toe sts tog.

Weave in all ends. ●

TIPS:

When beginning the cuff, cast on using a needle 2 to 3 sizes larger, then slip your stitches onto the correct size of double-point needles when setting up to knit your first round.

To avoid "toe ears" when working Kitchener stitch, begin with Step 3 of Kitchener instructions and slip remaining stitch off each needle after working Step 6.

Red Rock Sunset

Design by Jackie Daugherty

These socks reverse the standard stockinette stitching for a unique take on socks.

SKILL LEVEL
Intermediate

SIZE
Woman's small (medium, large); to fit shoe size 5 to 6 (7 to 8, 9 to 10).

Instructions are given for the smallest size, with larger sizes in parentheses. When only 1 number is given, it applies to all sizes.

FINISHED MEASUREMENT
Foot Circumference: 7 (7½, 8) inches

MATERIALS

- Lana Grossa Meilenweit Merino Sock (fingering weight; 80% merino, 20% nylon; 375 yds/95g per hank): 1 hank #408 tapi
- Size 1½ (2.5mm) double-point needles (set of 5) or size needed to obtain gauge
- Removable stitch marker
- Stitch holder

GAUGE
36 sts and 48 rows = 4 inches/10cm in Triangle pat, after blocking.

To save time, take time to check gauge.

PATTERN STITCHES
1x1 Rib (even number of sts)
All rnds: *K1, p1; rep from * around.

Triangle (multiple of 6 sts)
Note: *Chart is provided for those preferring to work Triangle pat from chart.*

Rnd 1: Knit.

Rnd 2: *P5, k1; rep from * around.

Rnd 3: *P4, k2; rep from * around.

Rnd 4: *P3, k3; rep from * around.

Rnd 5: *P2, k4; rep from * around.

Rnd 6: *P1, k5; rep from * around.

Rep Rnds 1–6 for pat.

STITCH KEY
☐ K
⊟ P

6-st rep

TRIANGLE CHART

SOCK
Make 2.

CUFF
Cast on 60 (66, 72) sts. Divide sts evenly among 3 dpns. Pm on first st of rnd and join to work in the rnd.

Beg 1x1 Rib; work 16 rnds even.

LEG
Change to Triangle pat; work [Rnds 1–6] 10 times.

Next rnd: Knit to last st; sl last st and following 30 (30, 36) sts to st holder for top of foot, removing beg-of-rnd marker—31 (31, 37) sts on st holder. Place rem 29 (35, 35) sts on 1 dpn for heel flap.

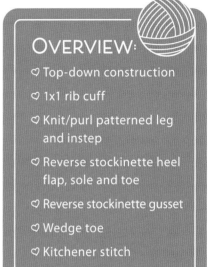

OVERVIEW:
- ♡ Top-down construction
- ♡ 1x1 rib cuff
- ♡ Knit/purl patterned leg and instep
- ♡ Reverse stockinette heel flap, sole and toe
- ♡ Reverse stockinette gusset
- ♡ Wedge toe
- ♡ Kitchener stitch

HEEL FLAP
Work back and forth in rows on 29 (35, 35) heel sts only.

Row 1 (WS): Sl 1 wyif, k26 (32, 32), p2tog—28 (34, 34) sts.

Row 2 (RS): Sl 1 wyib, p26 (32, 32), k1.

Row 3: Sl 1 wyif, k26 (32, 32) sts, p1.

Rep [Rows 2 and 3] 14 (15, 15) more times.

TURN HEEL
Row 1 (RS): Sl 1, p15 (18, 18), p2tog, p1, turn.

Row 2 (WS): Sl 1, k5, ssk, k1, turn.

Note: *There is now a gap between sts at each turning point.*

Row 3: Sl 1, purl to 1 st before gap, p2tog, p1, turn.

Row 4: Sl 1, knit to 1 st before gap, ssk, k1, turn.

Rep Rows 3 and 4 until all sts have been worked, ending with a WS row—16 (20, 20) sts.

Note: For size small, you will not have enough sts to work final p1 and k1 at end of last rep of Rows 3 and 4.

Next row: Purl.

GUSSET

Set-up rnd: Sl last 8 (10, 10) sts from heel flap to dpn (Needle 1), with same needle and RS of heel flap facing, pick up and knit 15 (16, 17) sts along side edge of heel flap; sl 31 (31, 37) sts from st holder to 2nd dpn (Needle 2) and knit 1, work Rnd 2 of Triangle pat to end of Needle 2; with 3rd dpn (Needle 3), pick up and knit 15 (16, 17) sts along opposite side edge of heel flap, then purl rem 8 (10, 10) sts from heel flap—77 (83, 91) sts; 23 (26, 27) sts on Needles 1 and 2, and 31 (31, 37) sts on Needle 2.

Note: New beg of rnd is at center of heel.

Rnd 1: Needle 1: Purl to end of needle; **Needle 2:** K1, work in Triangle pat to end of needle; **Needle 3:** Purl to end of needle.

Rnd 2: Needle 1: Purl to last 3 sts on needle, p2tog, p1; **Needle 2:** K1, work in Triangle pat to end of needle; **Needle 3:** P1, p2tog-tbl, purl to end of needle.

Rep [Rnds 1 and 2] 7 (9, 8) more times—61 (63, 73) sts; 15 (16, 18) sts on Needles 1 and 3, and 31 (31, 37) sts on Needle 2.

FOOT

Work even, purling all sts on Needles 1 and 3 and working in pat as established on Needle 2 until foot measures 7 (7½, 8) inches from back of heel, or to 2 inches shorter than desired length, ending with Rnd 6 of Triangle pat.

Next rnd: Needle 1: Purl to end of needle; **Needle 2:** K2tog, knit to end of needle; **Needle 3:** Purl to end of needle—60 (62, 72) sts; 15 (16, 18) sts on Needles 1 and 3, and 30 (30, 36) sts on Needle 2.

TOE

Rnd 1: Needle 1: Purl to last 3 sts on needle, p2tog, p1; **Needle 2:** P1, p2tog-tbl, purl to last 3 sts on needle, p2tog, p1; **Needle 3:** P1, p2tog-tbl, purl to end of needle—4 sts dec.

Rnd 2: Purl.

Rep [Rnds 1 and 2] 9 (9, 11) more times—20 (22, 24) sts.

With Needle 3, purl to end of Needle 1; rearrange sts if necessary so that you have the same number of sts on both needles.

FINISHING

Turn sock WS out and, using Kitchener stitch, graft toe sts tog. Weave in all ends. Turn RS out and block. ●

Frosty Woods

Design by Lena Skvagerson

The colorwork makes these an awesome addition to your Christmas wardrobe, and the toe-up technique gives you another opportunity to try something different.

SKILL LEVEL
Intermediate

SIZE
Woman's small (medium, large); to fit shoe size 5 to 6 (7 to 8, 9 to 10)

Instructions are given for the smallest size, with larger sizes in parentheses. When only 1 number is given, it applies to all sizes.

FINISHED MEASUREMENT
Foot Circumference: 7 (7, 8) inches

MATERIALS

- Rose Hill Yarns (fingering weight; 75% superwash merino/25% nylon yarn; 232 yds/50g per skein): 1 skein cranberry (B)
- Rose Hill Yarns (fingering weight; 75% superwash merino/25% nylon yarn; 116 yds/25g per skein): 2 skeins each dark leaf (A) and natural (C)
- Size 1½ (2.5mm) double-point needles (set of 5) or size needed to obtain gauge
- Removable stitch marker
- Stitch holder

GAUGE
32 sts and 44 rows = 4 inches/10cm in St st.

To save time, take time to check gauge.

SPECIAL ABBREVIATIONS
Make 1 Left (M1L): Insert LH needle from front to back under horizontal strand between last st worked and next st on LH needle; knit through back of resulting loop.

Make 1 Right (M1R): Insert LH needle from back to front under horizontal strand between last st worked and next st on LH needle; knit into front of resulting loop.

Wrap & Turn (W&T): On RS rows: Slip next st pwise to RH needle wyib. Bring yarn to RS of work between needles, then slip same st back to LH needle. Bring yarn to WS, wrapping st. Turn, leaving rem sts unworked, then beg working back in the other direction. **On WS rows:** Slip next st pwise to RH needle wyif. Bring yarn to RS of work between needles, then slip same st back to LH needle. Bring yarn to WS, wrapping st. Turn, leaving rem sts unworked, then beg working back in the other direction. **To hide wraps on subsequent rows:** Work to wrapped st. With RH needle, pick up wrap and work wrap tog with wrapped st.

PATTERN STITCHES
Foot (multiple of 8 sts)
Note: A chart is provided for those preferring to work pat st from a chart.

Rnd 1: *K1 C, k3 A; rep from * around.

Rnd 2: *K2 C, k1 A, k3 C, k1 A, k1 C; rep from * around.

Rnd 3: *K5 C, k1 B, k1 C, k1 B; rep from * around.

Rnd 4: *K1 B, k3 C, [k1 B, k1 C] twice; rep from * around.

Rnd 5: *K1 C, k1 B; rep from * around.

Rnd 6: *K1 B, k1 C; rep from * around.

Leg (multiple of 10 sts)
Note: A chart is provided for those preferring to work pat st from a chart.

Rnd 1: *K1 C, k1 B; rep from * around.

OVERVIEW:
- ♡ Toe-up construction
- ♡ Turkish cast-on
- ♡ Wedge toe
- ♡ Colorwork toe and leg
- ♡ Reverse gusset and heel flap
- ♡ Half twisted rib cuff
- ♡ Jeny's Surprisingly Stretchy Bind-Off

Rnd 2: Knit with C.

Rnd 3: *K1 B, k1 C; rep from * around.

Rnd 4: Knit with B.

Rnd 5: *K2 A, k2 B, k1 A, k1 B, k1 A, k2 B, k1 A; rep from * around.

Rnd 6: *K1 A, k3 B, k3 A, k3 B; rep from * around.

Rnd 7: *K4 B, k1 A, k1 B, k1 A, k3 B; rep from * around.

Rnd 8: *K1 B, k3 A, k1 B, k1 A, k1 B, k3 A; rep from * around.

Rnd 9: *K2 B, [k3 A, k1 B] twice; rep from * around.

Rnd 10: *K3 B, k5 A, k2 B; rep from * around.

Rnd 11: *K1 A, k3 B, k1 A, k1 B, k1 A, k3 B; rep from * around.

Rnd 12: *K2 B, k2 A, k1 B, k1 A, k1 B, k2 A, k1 B; rep from * around.

Rnd 13: *K3 B, k2 A, k1 B, k2 A, k2 B; rep from * around.

Rnd 14: *K1 B, k1 A, k2 B, k3 A, k2 B, k1 A; rep from * around.

Rnd 15: *K2 A, k3 B, k1 A, k3 B, k1 A; rep from * around.

Rnd 16: *K1 B, k1 A, k7 B, k1 A; rep from * around.

Rnd 17: *K1 A, k1 B, [k3 A, k1 B] twice; rep from * around.

Rnd 18: *K1 B, k3 A, k3 B, k3 A; rep from * around.

Rnd 19: *K3 A, k5 B, k2 A; rep from * around.

Rnd 20: *K1 B, k1 A, [k3 B, k1 A] twice; rep from * around.

Rnd 21: *K1 A, k1 B, k2 A, k3 B, k2 A, k1 B; rep from * around.

Rnd 22: *K1 B, k2 A, k5 B, k2 A; rep from * around.

Rnd 23: *K2 A, k2 B, k3 A, k2 B, k1 A; rep from * around.

Rnd 24: *K1 A, k4 B; rep from * around.

Rnd 25: Knit with B.

Rnd 26: *K2 B, [k1 C, k1 B] 4 times; rep from * around.

Rnd 27: Knit with B.

Rnd 28: *K1 B, k1 C; rep from * around.

Rnd 29: Knit with B.

Rnd 30: *K2 B, [k1 C, k1 B] 4 times; rep from * around.

Rnd 31: *K1 B, k1 C, k7 B, k1 C; rep from * around.

Rnd 32: *K1 C, k4 B; rep from * around.

Rnd 33: *K1 C, k3 B, k1 C, k1 B, k1 C, k3 B; rep from * around.

Rnd 34: *K1 C, k2 B, [k1 C, k1 B] twice, k1 C, k2 B; rep from * around.

Rnd 35: *K2 B, [k1 C, k1 B] 4 times; rep from * around.

Rnd 36: *K1 B, k1 C; rep from * around.

Cuff Ribbing

All rnds: *K1-tbl, p1; rep from * around.

SOCK

Make 2.

TOE

Using 2 dpns held tog, Turkish cast-on and A, cast on 24 sts, 12 sts onto each dpn.

Rnd 1: Knit.

Rnd 2: *K1, M1L, k10, M1R, k1, pm; rep from * once more—28 sts.

Divide sts evenly onto 4 dpns.

Rnd 3: Knit.

Rnd 4: Needle 1: K1, M1R, knit to end of needle; Needle 2: Knit to last st, on needle, M1L, k1; Needles 3 and 4: Work as for Needles 1 and 2—4 sts inc.

Rep [Rnds 3 and 4] 6 (6, 8) more times—56 (56, 64) sts.

FOOT

Rnds 1–6: Work Rnds 1–6 of Foot pat. Cut A and C.

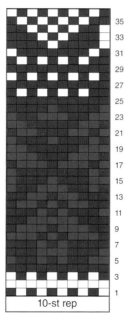

LEG CHART

COLOR KEY
- A
- B
- C

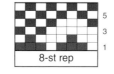

8-st rep

FOOT CHART

Note: Knit on RS; purl on WS.

Continuing in B, work in St st (knit every rnd) until piece measures approx 5 (5, 5¾) inches from tip of toe, or to 4 (4½, 4¼) inches shorter than desired length.

GUSSET

Inc rnd: Needles 1 and 2: Knit; **Needle 3:** K1, M1R, knit to end of needle; **Needle 4:** Knit to last st, M1L, k1—2 sts inc.

Next rnd: Knit.

Rep last 2 rnds 10 (12, 10) more times—78 (82, 86) sts; 14 (14, 16) instep sts each on Needles 1 and 2 and 25 (27, 27) sole sts each on Needles 3 and 4.

Size Medium Only

Redistribute sts so there are 15 instep sts each on Needles 1 and 2 and 26 sole sts each on Needles 3 and 4.

All Sizes

Next rnd: Work to end of Needle 2 and place 28 (30, 32) sts from Needles 1 and 2 on st holder.

TURN HEEL

With A, work back and forth in short rows over 50 (52, 54) sole sts.

Short row 1 (RS): Knit to last 12 sts, W&T.

Short row 2 (WS): Purl to last 12 sts, W&T—26 (28, 30) sts in center between wrapped st on each side.

Note: There is now a gap between sts at each turning point.

Short row 3: Knit to 1 st before wrapped st from previous RS row, W&T.

Short row 4: Purl to 1 st before wrapped st from previous WS row, W&T—24 (26, 28) sts in center between wrapped sts on each side.

Rep [Short rows 3 and 4] 8 (9, 10) more times—8 sts in center between wrapped sts on each side; 10 (11, 12) wrapped sts on each side; 11 sts between last wrapped st and end of needle on each side.

Short row 5 (RS): K8, knit 10 (11, 12) wrapped sts (hiding wraps), turn, leaving last 11 sts unworked.

Short row 6: Sl 1 pwise wyif, purl to first wrapped st, purl 10 (11, 12) wrapped sts (hiding wraps), turn, leaving last 11 sts unworked.

HEEL FLAP

Row 1 (RS): Sl 1 kwise wyib, knit to 1 st before gap, ssk, turn, leaving rem sts unworked—1 st dec.

Row 2 (WS): Sl 1 pwise wyif, purl to 1 st before gap, p2tog, turn, leaving rem sts unworked—1 st dec.

Rep [Rows 1 and 2] 10 more times—28 (30, 32) sts.

Return held 28 (30, 32) instep sts to 2 needles—56 (60, 64) sts.

LEG

Change to B and knit 5 (7, 7) rnds.

Size Small Only

Next rnd: *M1R, k14; rep from * around—60 sts.

Size Large Only

Next rnd: *K2tog, k14; rep from * around—60 sts.

All Sizes

Rnds 1–36: Work Rnds 1–36 of Leg pat.

Rnd 37: With C, knit.

Rnds 38 and 39: With B, knit.

CUFF

Rnd 1: With A, knit.

Work Cuff Ribbing until cuff measures approx 1¼ inches.

Cut A.

With B, knit 2 rnds.

Bind-off rnd: K1, *backward yo (bringing yarn from back to front over RH needle), k1, pass yo and first st on RH needle over last st (1 st bound off, 1 st left on RH needle); rep from * until all sts are bound off.

FINISHING

Weave in all ends. ●

COLORWORK TIPS:

You may find that when you work the colorwork section, your gauge tightens up. Many knitters find it helpful to work colorwork sections on a needle 1 size larger to keep the stitching even across the entire piece.

When one color stands out more than another in a piece, that color is dominant. When working colorwork you may find you get nicer, more even stitches if you work your dominant color a particular way consistently throughout. Generally, if you are working colorwork two-handed, and you start with one color in your left hand, keep it there throughout. If you are working one-handed, and you keep that yarn as the upper yarn, keep it there throughout.

Swatching is your friend with colorwork. It will give you practice with your floats, changing colors and determining dominant color.

Twined Vines

Design by Lena Skvagerson

These super stretchy socks have a very unique
heck design that you must try!

SKILL LEVEL
Intermediate

SIZE
Woman's small/medium (medium/
large); to fit shoe size 5 to 8 (8 to 11)

Instructions are given for the smaller
size, with larger size in parentheses.
When only 1 number is given, it
applies to both sizes.

FINISHED MEASUREMENT
Foot circumference: 7 (7¾) inches

MATERIALS

- Lana Grossa
  Meilenweit Merino
  Sock (fingering
  weight; 80% merino/20%
  nylon; 375 yds/95g per skein):
  1 skein #308 nanda
- Size 1½ (2.5mm) double-
  point needles (set of 4) or size
  needed to obtain gauge
- Removable stitch marker
- Cable needle
- Stitch holder

GAUGE
32 sts and 40 rnds = 4 inches/10cm in
St st.

To save time, take time to check gauge.

SPECIAL ABBREVIATIONS
3 over 3 Left Ribbed Cross (3/3 LRC):
Sl 3 sts to cn and hold in front; p1, k1,
p1, then p1, k1, p1 from cn.

**3 over 3 Right Ribbed Cross (3/3
RRC):** Sl 3 sts to cn and hold in back;
p1, k1, p1, then p1, k1, p1 from cn.

Centered Double Decrease (CDD):
Sl 2 sts as if to k2tog, k1, p2sso to dec
2 sts.

Make 1 Left (M1L): Insert LH needle
from front to back under horizontal
strand between last st worked and
next st on LH needle; knit through
back of resulting loop.

Make 1 Purlwise (M1P): Insert LH
needle from back to front under
horizontal strand between last st
worked and next st on LH needle; purl
into front of resulting loop.

Make 1 Right (M1R): Insert LH needle
from back to front under horizontal
strand between last st worked and
next st on LH needle; knit into front
of resulting loop.

OVERVIEW:
- ♡ Top-down construction
- ♡ 1x1 rib and cable rib leg
- ♡ Reverse Fleegle heel
- ♡ Cable rib instep
- ♡ Wedge toe
- ♡ Cinched toe closure

PATTERN STITCH
Criss Cross Cables
[multiple of 6 sts + 3]

Rnds 1–6: *P1, k1, p1; rep from * to end.

Rnd 7: *3/3 LRC; rep from * to last 3 sts, p1, k1, p1.

Rnds 8–13: Rep Rnds 1–6.

Rnd 14: P1, k1, p1, *3/3 RRC; rep from * to end.

Rep Rnds 1–14 for pat.

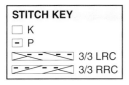

CRISS CROSS CABLES CHART

SOCK
Make 2.

LEG
Cast on 70 (80) sts. Divide sts among 3 dpns, as follows: 16 (18) sts on Needle 1, 15 (17) sts on Needle 2 and 39 (45) sts on Needle 3. Pm on first st of rnd and join to work in the rnd.

Rnd 1: Needles 1 and 2: *K1, p1; rep from * to last st on Needle 2, k1; **Needle 3:** Work Rnd 1 of Criss Cross Cables.

Rnd 2: Needles 1 and 2: Work in 1x1 rib as established; **Needle 3:** Work next rnd in Criss Cross Cables.

Rep Rnd 2 until you have worked Rnds 1–14 of Criss Cross Cables a total of 4 times, then rep [Rnd 2] 0 (7) more times.

HEEL FLAP
Rnd 1: Needles 1 and 2: K1, M1L, p1, *k1, p1; rep from * to last st on Needle 2, M1R, k1; **Needle 3:** Work in Criss Cross Cables as established—1 st inc each on Needles 1 and 2.

Rnd 2: Needles 1 and 2: K2, p1, *k1, p1; rep from * to last 2 sts on Needle 2, k2; **Needle 3:** Work Criss Cross Cables.

Rnd 3: Needles 1 and 2: K1, M1P, *k1, p1; rep from * to last 2 sts on Needle 2, k1, M1P, k1; **Needle 3:** Work Criss Cross Cables—1 st inc each on Needles 1 and 2.

Rnd 4: Needles 1 and 2: *K1, p1; rep from * to last st on Needle 2, k1; **Needle 3:** Work Criss Cross Cables.

Rep [Rnds 1–4] 6 (7) more times—59 (67) sts; 30 (34) sts on Needle 1, 29 (33) sts on Needle 2 and 39 (45) sts on Needle 3.

Heel Turn
Work back and forth in rows on 59 (67) sts on Needles 1 and 2 only; leave 39 (45) sts on Needle 3 for instep.

Row 1 (RS): Sl 1, k30 (34) sts, ssk, k1.

Row 2 (WS): Sl 1, p4, p2tog, p1, turn.

Note: There is now a gap between sts at each turning point.

Row 3: Sl 1, knit to 1 st before gap, ssk, k1, turn.

Row 4: Sl 1, purl to 1 st before gap, p2tog, p1, turn.

Rep Rows 3 and 4 until all sts have been worked—31 (35) sts.

FOOT
Next rnd: Needles 1 and 2: Knit; **Needle 3:** Work Criss Cross Cables—70 (80) sts.

Work even, working St st on Needles 1 and 2 and Criss Cross Cables on Needle 3, until foot measures 7 (8) inches from back of heel or to approx 2 (2¼) inches less than desired length.

TOE
Rearrange sts so that you have 17 (19) sts on Needle 1, 18 (20) sts on Needle 2 and 35 (39) sts on Needle 3.

Rnd 1: Needle 1: K1, ssk, knit to end on needle; **Needle 2:** Knit to last 3 sts on needle, k2tog, k1; **Needle 3:** K1, ssk, knit to last 3 sts, k2tog, k1—4 sts dec.

Rep Rnd 1 every other rnd twice, then every rnd 12 (15) times—10 (8) sts.

Size Small/Medium Only
Next rnd: K1, CDD, k2, CDD, k1—6 sts.

Size Medium/Large Only
Next rnd: K1, k2tog, k2, k2tog, k1—6 sts.

All Sizes
Cut yarn, leaving a 6-inch tail. Thread tail through rem sts and pull tight to close.

FINISHING
Weave in all ends. ●

> **TIP:**
>
> This sock is extremely stretchy. Try it on periodically and check the fit. You can decrease the leg to be fewer stitches but you will then need to be able to do the math to adjust the heel instructions accordingly.

Victoriana

Design by Lena Skvagerson

These socks will keep you on your toes with the many different lace stitch patterns used. This pattern requires focus but is totally worth the effort.

SKILL LEVEL

Intermediate

SIZE

Woman's small (medium, large); to fit shoe size 5 to 6 (7 to 8, 9 to 10)

Instructions are given for the smallest size, with larger sizes in parentheses. When only 1 number is given, it applies to all sizes.

FINISHED MEASUREMENT

Foot Circumference: 7½ (8, 8½) inches

MATERIALS

- SpaceCadet® Celeste (fingering weight; 100% superwash merino wool; 490 yds/100g per skein): 1 skein faded promises
- Size 1½ (2.5mm) double-point needles (set of 5) or size needed to obtain gauge
- Removable stitch marker
- Stitch holder

GAUGE

32 sts and 44 rows = 4 inches/10cm in St st.

To save time, take time to check gauge.

SPECIAL ABBREVIATIONS

Centered Double Decrease (CDD): Sl 2 sts as if to k2tog, k1, p2sso to dec 2 sts.

Make 1 Left (M1L): Insert LH needle from front to back under horizontal strand between last st worked and next st on LH needle; knit into back of resulting loop.

PATTERN STITCHES

Note: Charts are provided for those preferring to work pat sts from a chart.

Cuff Lace (panel of 21 sts)

Rnd 1: *K3, yo, k1, yo, k3, sk2p, k2, k3tog, k3, yo, k1, yo, k2; rep from * around.

Rnd 2 and all even-numbered rnds: Knit.

Rnd 3: *K2, yo, k1, yo, k3, sk2p, k4, k3tog, k3, [yo, k1] twice; rep from * around.

Rnd 5: *[K1, yo] twice, k3, sk2p, k6, k3tog, k3, yo, k1, yo; rep from * around.

Rnd 7: Rep Rnd 3.

Rnd 9: Rep Rnd 1.

Rnd 11: *K4, yo, k1, yo, k3, sk2p, k3tog, k3, yo, k1, yo, k3; rep from * around.

Rnd 12: Knit.

Rep Rnds 1–12 for pat.

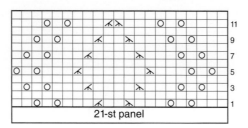

21-st panel

CUFF LACE CHART

STITCH KEY

□	K
☉	Yo
⊼	K3tog
⋌	Sk2p

Diamond Lace (panel of 15 sts)

Rnd 1: K4, k2tog, k1, [yo, k1] twice, ssk, k4.

Rnd 2 and all even-numbered rnds: Knit.

Rnd 3: K3, k2tog, k1, yo, k3, yo, k1, ssk, k3.

Rnd 5: K2, k2tog, k1, yo, k5, yo, k1, ssk, k2.

Rnd 7: K1, k2tog, k1, yo, k7, yo, k1, ssk, k1.

Rnd 9: K2tog, k1, yo, k2, ssk, yo, k1, yo, k2tog, k2, yo, k1, ssk.

Rnd 11: K2, yo, k2tog, ssk, yo, k3, yo, k2tog, ssk, yo, k2.

Rnd 13: K3, [yo, k2tog] twice, k1, [ssk, yo] twice, k3.

Rnd 15: K4, yo, ssk, yo, CDD, yo, k2tog, yo, k4.

Rnd 17: K5, yo, ssk, k1, k2tog, yo, k5.

Rnd 19: K6, yo, CDD, yo, k6.

Rnd 21: Knit.

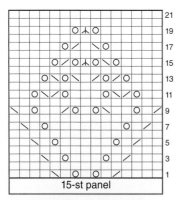

DIAMOND LACE CHART

STITCH KEY
- ☐ K
- ⊡ Yo
- ⊿ K2tog
- ◺ Ssk
- ⊼ CDD

Wide Fern Lace (panel of 21 sts)

Rnd 1: K3, [ssk, k1] twice, [yo, k1] 4 times, k2tog, k1, k2tog, k3.

Rnd 2 and all even-numbered rnds: Knit.

Rnd 3: K2, [ssk, k1] twice, yo, k1, yo, k3, [yo, k1] twice, k2tog, k1, k2tog, k2.

Rnd 5: K1, [ssk, k1] twice, yo, k1, yo, k5, [yo, k1] twice, k2tog, k1, k2tog, k1.

Rnd 7: [Ssk, k1] twice, yo, k1, yo, k7, [yo, k1] twice, k2tog, k1, k2tog.

Rnd 8: Knit.

Rep Rnds 1–8 for pat.

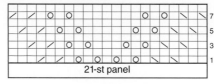

WIDE FERN LACE CHART

STITCH KEY
- ☐ K
- ⊡ Yo
- ⊿ K2tog
- ◺ Ssk

Right Fern Lace (panel of 11 sts)

Row/Rnd 1 (RS): K3, [ssk, k1] twice, [yo, k1] twice.

Row/Rnd 2 and all even-numbered rows/rnds: Knit on RS, purl on WS.

Row/Rnd 3: K2, [ssk, k1] twice, yo, k1, yo, k2.

Row/Rnd 5: [K1, ssk] twice, [k1, yo] twice, k3.

Row/Rnd 7: [Ssk, k1] twice, yo, k1, yo, k4.

Row/Rnd 8: Knit on RS, purl on WS.

Rep Rows/Rnds 1–8 for pat.

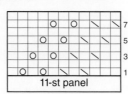

RIGHT FERN LACE CHART

STITCH KEY
- ☐ K on RS, p on WS
- ⊡ Yo
- ◺ Ssk

Left Fern Lace (panel of 11 sts)

Row/Rnd 1 (RS): [K1, yo] twice, [k1, k2tog] twice, k3.

Row/Rnd 2 and all even-numbered rows/rnds: Knit on RS, purl on WS.

Row/Rnd 3: K2, [yo, k1] twice, k2tog, k1, k2tog, k2.

Row/Rnd 5: K3, [yo, k1] twice, [k2tog, k1] twice.

Row/Rnd 7: K4, [yo, k1] twice, k2tog, k1, k2tog.

Row/Rnd 8: Knit on RS, purl on WS.

Rep Rows 1–8 for pat.

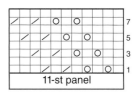

LEFT FERN LACE CHART

STITCH KEY
- ☐ K on RS, p on WS
- ⊡ Yo
- ⊿ K2tog

RIGHT SOCK

CUFF

Loosely cast on 84 sts. Divide sts evenly among 4 dpns (21 sts per needle). Pm on first st of rnd and join to work in the rnd.

Knit 1 rnd, purl 1 rnd, knit 1 rnd.

Work Cuff Lace for 36 rnds.

Size Small Only

Next rnd: *K1, ssk, k4, [ssk] twice, [k2tog] twice, k4, k2tog; rep from * around—60 sts.

Size Medium Only

Next rnd: *K1, ssk, k4, ssk, k1, k2tog, k1, k2tog, k4, k2tog; rep from * around—64 sts.

Size Large Only

Next rnd: *K1, [ssk, k4] twice, k2tog, k4, k2tog; rep from * around—68 sts.

All Sizes

Work 10 (12, 15) rnds in St st (knit every rnd).

Sl 15 (16, 17) sts from Needles 1 and 2 onto 1 dpn [this is now Needle 1; 30 (32, 34) sts]; leave 15 (16, 17) sts each on 2 dpns (these are now Needles 2 and 3).

Diamond Lace

Rnd 1: K8 (9, 10), work Rnd 1 of Diamond Lace over 15 sts, knit to end of rnd.

Rnds 2–19: K8 (9, 10), work next rnd of Diamond Lace, knit to end of rnd.

Rnds 20 and 21: Knit.

Wide Fern Lace

Rnd 1: K5 (6, 7), work Rnd 1 of Wide Fern Lace over 21 sts, knit to end of rnd.

Rnds 2–16: K5 (6, 7), work next rnd of Wide Fern Lace, knit to end of rnd.

HEEL FLAP

Row 1 (RS): K5 (6, 7), work Row 1 of Right Fern Lace over 11 sts, M1L, sl next 29 (31, 33) sts onto st holder for instep, then sl last 15 (16, 17) sts onto end of Needle 1 for heel flap.

Work back and forth in rows on 32 (34, 36) heel flap sts only.

Row 2 (WS): Sl 1, work next row of Right Fern Lace over 11 sts, purl to end.

Row 3: Sl 1, knit to last 12 sts, work next row of Right Fern Lace to last st, k1.

Row 4: Rep Row 2.

Rows 5–24: Rep [Rows 3 and 4] 10 times.

Row 25: Sl 1, knit to end.

Row 26: Sl 1, purl to end.

Rep [Rows 25 and 26] 2 (3, 4) more times.

Next row (RS): Sl 1, k2tog, knit to last 2 sts, ssk—30 (32, 34) sts.

Turn Heel

Row 1 (WS): Sl 1, p16 (18, 18), p2tog, p1, turn.

Row 2 (RS): Sl 1, k5 (7, 5), ssk, k1, turn.

Note: There is now a gap between sts at each turning point.

Row 3: Sl 1, purl to 1 st before gap, p2tog, p1, turn.

Row 4: Sl 1, knit to 1 st before gap, ssk, k1, turn.

Rep Rows 3 and 4 until all sts have been worked, ending with a RS row; do not turn on final row—18 (20, 20) sts.

GUSSET

Rnd 1 (RS): Sl last 9 (10, 10) sts onto dpn (Needle 1). With RS of heel flap facing, using same needle, pick up and knit 16 (16, 17) sts along side edge of heel flap; with Needle 2, work as follows across 29 (31, 33) sts from st holder for instep: M1L, [yo, k1] twice, k2tog, k1, k2tog, k22 (24, 26); with Needle 3, pick up and knit 16 (16, 17) sts along opposite side edge of heel flap, then knit across rem 9 (10, 10) sts from heel flap—80 (84, 88) sts; 25 (26, 27) sts on Needles 1 and 3, and 30 (32, 34) sts on Needle 2.

Note: Pm for new beg of rnd at center of heel.

Rnd 2: Needle 1: Knit to end of needle; **Needle 2:** Work Rnd 2 of Left Fern Lace over 11 sts, knit to end of needle; **Needle 3:** Knit to end.

Rnd 3: Needle 1: Knit to last 3 sts on needle, k2tog, k1; **Needle 2:** Work next rnd of Left Fern Lace over 11 sts, knit to end of needle; **Needle 3:** K1, ssk, knit to end—1 st dec each on Needles 1 and 3.

Rnd 4: Needles 1 and 3: Knit; **Needle 2:** Work next rnd of Left Fern Lace over 11 sts, knit to end.

Rnds 5–22: Rep [Rnds 3 and 4] 9 times—60 (64, 68) sts; 15 (16, 17) sts each on Needles 1 and 3, and 30 (32, 34) sts on Needle 2.

Rnds 23–40: Needles 1 and 3: Knit; **Needle 2:** Work next rnd of Left Fern Lace over 11 sts, knit to end.

FOOT

Change to St st across all sts; work even until foot measures 7¼ (7¾, 8¼) inches from back of heel or to 1¾ inches shorter than desired length.

TOE

Rnd 1: Needle 1: Knit to last 3 sts on needle, k2tog, k1; **Needle 2:** K1, ssk, knit to last 3 sts on needle, k2tog, k1; **Needle 3:** K1, ssk, knit to end—4 sts dec.

Rnd 2: Knit.

Rep [Rnds 1 and 2] 9 times—20 (24, 28) sts.

With Needle 3, knit across 5 (6, 7) sts from Needle 1.

FINISHING

Cut yarn, leaving a 12-inch tail.

Using Kitchener stitch, graft toe sts tog.

Weave in all ends.

LEFT SOCK

Work as for right sock to beg of heel flap.

HEEL FLAP

Row 1 (RS): K5 (6, 7), work Rnd 1 of Wide Fern Lace over 21 sts, k19 (21, 23), sl next 30 (32, 34) sts onto st holder for instep, removing beg-of-rnd marker, then slip rem 30 (32, 34) sts onto 1 dpn for heel flap.

Work back and forth in rows on 30 (32, 34) heel sts only.

Row 2 (WS): Sl 1, purl to end, M1L— 31 (33, 35) sts.

Row 3: Sl 1, work Row 3 of Left Fern Lace over 11 sts, knit to end of row.

Row 4: Sl 1, purl to last 12 sts, work next row of Right Fern Lace to last st, p1.

Row 5: Sl 1, work next row of Left Fern Lace over 11 sts, knit to end of row.

Rows 6–23: Rep [Rows 4 and 5] 9 times.

Row 24: Rep Row 4.

Row 25: Sl 1, knit to end.

Row 26: Sl 1, purl to end.

Rep [Rows 25 and 26] 2 (3, 4) more times.

Next row (RS): Sl 1, k2tog, knit to end—30 (32, 34) sts.

Turn Heel as for right sock.

GUSSET

Rnd 1: Sl last 9 (10, 10) sts onto dpn (Needle 1). With RS of heel flap facing, using same needle, pick up and knit 16 (16, 17) sts along side edge of heel flap; with Needle 2, work as follows across 30 (32, 34) sts from st holder for instep: K2tog, knit to end of needle, M1L; with Needle 3, pick up and knit 16 (16, 17) sts along opposite side edge of heel flap, then knit across rem 9 (10, 10) sts from heel flap—80 (84, 88) sts; 25 (26, 27) sts each on Needles 1 and 3, and 30 (32, 34) sts on Needle 2.

Note: Pm for new beg of rnd at center of heel.

Rnd 2: Needle 1: Knit to last 3 sts on needle, k2tog, k1; **Needle 2:** K18 (20, 22), work Rnd 3 of Right Fern Lace over 11 sts, k1; **Needle 3:** K1, ssk, knit to end—78 (82, 86) sts; 24 (25, 26) sts each on Needles 1 and 3, and 30 (32, 34) sts on Needle 2.

Rnd 3: Needles 1 and 3: Knit; **Needle 2:** K18 (20, 22), work next rnd of Right Fern Lace over next 11 sts, k1.

Rnd 4: Needle 1: Knit to last 3 sts on needle, k2tog, k1; **Needle 2:** K18 (20, 22), work next rnd of Right Fern Lace over 11 sts, k1; **Needle 3:** K1, ssk, knit to end—1 st dec each on Needles 1 and 3.

Rnd 5: Rep Rnd 3.

Rnds 6–21: Rep [Rnds 4 and 5] 8 times—60 (64, 68) sts; 15 (16, 17) sts each on Needles 1 and 3, and 30 (32, 34) sts on Needle 2.

Rnds 22–39: Needles 1 and 3: Knit; **Needle 2:** K18 (20, 22), work next rnd of Right Fern Lace over 11 sts, k1.

Complete as for right sock.

TIPS:

Track where you are in the pattern carefully.

Use stitch markers to denote lace sections and to count rows to help track your progress.

![Annie's] Published by Annie's, 306 East Parr Road, Berne, IN 46711. Printed in USA. Copyright © 2024 Annie's. All rights reserved. This publication may not be reproduced in part or in whole without written permission from the publisher.

RETAIL STORES: If you would like to carry this publication or any other Annie's publication, visit AnniesWSL.com.

Every effort has been made to ensure that the instructions in this publication are complete and accurate. We cannot, however, take responsibility for human error, typographical mistakes or variations in individual work. Please visit AnniesCustomerService.com to check for pattern updates.

ISBN: 979-8-89253-371-3

1 2 3 4 5 6 7 8 9